Dante's
INFERNO

NOTES

Edited and with an Introduction by
HAROLD BLOOM

Printed and bound in the United States of America.

First Printing
1 3 5 7 9 8 6 4 2

ISBN: 0-7910-4086-0

Chelsea House Publishers
1974 Sproul Road, Suite 400
P.O. Box 914
Broomall, PA 19008-0914

Contents

User's Guide

This volume is designed to present biographical, critical, and bibliographical information on Dante and the *Inferno*. Following Harold Bloom's introduction, there appears a detailed biography of the author, discussing the major events in his life and his important literary works. Then follows a thematic and structural analysis of the work, in which significant themes, patterns, and motifs are traced. An annotated list of characters supplies brief information on the chief characters in the work.

A selection of critical extracts, derived from previously published material by leading critics, then follows. The extracts consist of statements by the author on his work, early reviews of the work, and later evaluations down to the present day. The items are arranged chronologically by date of first publication. A bibliography of Dante's writings (including publications from the invention of printing to the present day), a list of additional books and articles on him and on the *Inferno*, and an index of themes and ideas conclude the volume.

Harold Bloom is Sterling Professor of the Humanities at Yale University and Henry W. and Albert A. Berg Professor of English at the New York University Graduate School. He is the author of twenty books and the editor of more than thirty anthologies of literature and literary criticism.

Professor Bloom's works include *Shelley's Mythmaking* (1959), *The Visionary Company* (1961), *Blake's Apocalypse* (1963), *Yeats* (1970), *A Map of Misreading* (1975), *Kabbalah and Criticism* (1975), and *Agon: Towards a Theory of Revisionism* (1982). *The Anxiety of Influence* (1973) sets forth Professor Bloom's provocative theory of the literary relationships between the great writers and their predecessors. His most recent books are *The American Religion* (1992) and *The Western Canon* (1994).

Professor Bloom earned his Ph.D. from Yale University in 1955 and has served on the Yale faculty since then. He is a 1985 MacArthur Foundation Award recipient and served as the Charles Eliot Norton Professor of Poetry at Harvard University in 1987–88. He is currently the editor of the Chelsea House series Major Literary Characters and Modern Critical Views, and other Chelsea House series in literary criticism.

Introduction

HAROLD BLOOM

For most among us now, *The Divine Comedy* is an authentically difficult poem, which increases in its demands as we read on from the *Inferno* through the *Purgatorio* to the *Paradiso*. Yet even in translation, the astonishing power of the poem transcends what seem, to most of us, its awesome complexities. We do best to read it as story, even though it necessarily insists that it is not a fiction. For Dante, his poem was a new, apocalyptic Scripture, not replacing the two Testaments, but augmenting them. Essentially *The Divine Comedy* was intended as a prophecy, whose fulfillment Dante expected to see in his own lifetime. In his *Convivio* he had established the "perfect" human age as eighty-one, yet even had he not died at fifty-six, another quarter-century would only have further thwarted his expectations. The death of the Holy Roman Emperor Henry VII in 1313, before he could march upon Florence, had ended Dante's political hopes, which were intimately intertwined with his prophecy, though they formed only a part of the revelation that the poet considered he had been called upon to proclaim. We tend to be too much influenced by the Dante scholars who insist that Dante centered upon following the "allegory of the theologians," and who therefore make *The Divine Comedy* into versified St. Augustine. Manifestly, Dante possessed his own vision, distinct and original, and this proudest, hardest, and most ambitious of all Western poets scarcely was content to be any man's follower. A great prophet, be he Muhammad or Dante, is also a seer and a revelator, with a truth altogether his own that he must communicate. *The Divine Comedy,* like the *Koran,* intends Scriptural eminence. Pious Dante scholars find such a notion blasphemous, but it was not blasphemy to Dante.

This is not to say that Dante had no secular model for his poem; Virgil's *Aeneid* is the chosen precursor work, and clearly is surpassed by *The Divine Comedy*. But it is not sufficient to regard Dante's epic as simply the greatest work in that Western genre, at least since Homer. Like Milton's *Paradise Lost,* the *Comedy* is an intensely personal poem, and indeed is in one sense far more personal, since Dante the Pilgrim is the work's protagonist. Even though Dante the Poet-Prophet to some degree must be distinguished from Dante the Pilgrim, the two fuse together on the other side of the *Paradiso,* as it were. Dante is no Everyman, nor is he to be confounded with the wayfaring Christian of Bunyan's *Pilgrim's Progress.* Dante knows himself to be unique, and his poem demonstrates his election. He did not regard himself as less a prophet than Isaiah or Jeremiah or Ezekiel, and this profound self-awareness is a strong element of meaning in his poem. We may not be able to decipher his prophecy fully: there are unsolved mysteries in the poem, and some of them seem to have been coded by Dante in order to make them all but impossible to unravel. We need not solve all of them in order to read the poem, and participate in its magnificence. It is important though never to forget that Dante was as independent a poet as he was a human being. His intransigence kept him exiled from Florence for nearly the last two decades of his life. Whatever the personal cost of his unbending stance, he turns it to superb utility in a poem whose only aesthetic rivals are Homer and Shakespeare.

The *Inferno* doubtless always will be the most famous and most frequently read part of *The Divine Comedy.* Strictly speaking, the *Inferno* comprises Cantos III–XXXIV of the poem, since the first two cantos are introductory, and we pass through the gate of Hell in Canto III. Still, the poet's bewilderment and discouragement in the two opening cantos constitute a kind of internal inferno, and so it is all too natural to consider them as part of what so directly follows. Dante's self-representation in the first two cantos introduces one of the poem's most dramatic ironies; only he can undergo change in the poem, because he alone is a living mortal. Every other human being in the poem has died and undergone judgment, and so has become what always he or she is going to be. It is true that there is development in Purgatory, and even something like further refinement in Paradise, but neither of these involve change in the normal human sense. And in Hell, everything is absolutely fixed: no change can come. Nothing more will unfold, and so Dante's characters can reveal themselves absolutely by what they do and say. Fulfillment has come, though it be damnation.

This affords Dante the possibility that he so greatly exploits, particularly with the *Inferno*. We are given the *whole* story, whether it be of Ulysses, Farinata, Paolo and Francesca, Brunetto Latini, Ugolino, or all the other great personages of Hell. Total revelation is achieved. And yet, by a terrible irony, such revelation is achieved *despite* the characters rendered by Dante. As inhabitants of Hell, they are all petrified interpreters of their own situations, to borrow a grand insight from John Freccero, the most distinguished of living Dante critics. The interpretations they themselves offer throw frightening illuminations upon the views we all of us take of our own lives, our own dilemmas. There are countless values of increased consciousness to be gained by reading and pondering Dante's *Inferno*, yet I sometimes think that this is the strongest benefit Dante awards us. Where, in his Hell or in his Purgatory, do we belong, and how would he envision us if we were there? ✤

Biography of Dante

Dante Alighieri was born in May 1265 in the Italian city-state of Florence. Though little concrete information exists about his life, it appears that his family belonged to the Guelph party, which opposed the Ghibellines and their German allies. When Dante was a child, his mother died, and his father remarried and had several more children. Although the family was not wealthy, his father, who may have been a judge and a notary, was able to provide an education for his son; Dante attended school and may have studied rhetoric with Brunetto Latini.

According to his *Vita nuova* (The New Life), Dante taught himself to write verse at an early age. Poet Guido Cavalcanti befriended the youth and offered him guidance in his writing. Dante's first poems centered around his love for Beatrice, a beautiful Florentine noblewoman commonly believed to be Bice Portinari, whom he met when he was nine and she was eight; Dante loved and idolized her until her death in 1290. As he continued his education, reading such masters as Cicero and Aristotle, he shifted his poetic focus from courtly love to philosophy, the "mistress of his mind."

While developing his interest in poetry and philosophy, Dante assumed more worldly responsibilities as well. Before his father died in 1283, he arranged Dante's marriage to Gemma de Manetto Donati. The couple had two sons, Pietro and Jacopo—who later both wrote commentaries on *La Divina Commedia* (The Divine Comedy)—and at least one daughter. In 1289, Dante may have fought on the Guelph side at the battle of Campaldino, and he claims to have witnessed the surrender of the Pisan garrison of Caprona later that year. In any case, he expressed deep interest in the political conflicts of the time, opposing the efforts of Pope Boniface VIII to bring Florence and the rest of Tuscany under church control.

In 1295, Dante became actively involved in politics. Since guild membership was a requirement for political participation, he enrolled himself in the Guild of Physicians and Apothecaries and sought a role in the Florence government. He served on several councils, including the Consiglio dei Cento (Council of the Hundred) in 1296 and 1301, and was sent as ambassador to San Gimignano in 1300 to encourage opposition to the pope. Later that year he was elected to a two-month term in high office as one of Florence's six priors.

Political turmoil soon brought Dante's political career to a close. In 1301 he was one of three ambassadors for the Bianchi (the Whites) to travel on a diplomatic mission to Pope Boniface's court. While Dante was detained in Rome, French prince Charles of Valois assisted the Neri (the Blacks) in bringing Florence under papal control. In the wake of their victory, the Neri plundered Dante's home, as well as those of many other Bianchi. Accused of various trumped-up charges, Dante and other papal opponents were sentenced to exile from Florence.

Dante was never able to return to Florence, and it is unlikely he ever saw his wife again. He wandered extensively through Italy and probably visited Paris and Bologna, but his connection to Florence never ended. When Emperor Henry VII sought to restore order in Italy in 1310, Dante composed several epistles to support him. Around this time he probably also wrote his three-volume Latin treatise *De Monarchia* (On World Government), in which he argued that the rule of a monarchy is necessary for peace; that imperial authority rests with the Romans, specifically the Holy Roman Emperor; and that the authority of the Roman emperor is derived directly from God, independent of the pope. The work was condemned by the church, and Dante's hopes for imperial rule in Florence ended when Henry VII died in 1313. After obtaining refuge for a time with Can Grande della Scala in Verona, Dante secured the protection of Guido Novello da Polenta in Ravenna, where he remained until his death in September 1321.

By the time he arrived in Ravenna, Dante had earned a reputation as an accomplished poet. Sometime between 1292 and 1300, he composed *Vita nuova*, gathering poems he had written in the previous decade and creating bridges of narrative prose between them to give the verse a new order and meaning. An early example of Italian literary prose, *Vita nuova* revolves around the poet, Beatrice, and the Lord of Love in a story of idealized romance. Other poems from this period have been published in a collection titled *Rime* or *Canzoniere* (Lyric Poetry).

After 1304, Dante's work exhibited a more philosophical bent. The canzones in *Convivio* (The Banquet) concern love and virtue but also contain prose essays expounding their allegorical and religious significance. Dante planned to comment on fourteen of his long poems but only completed three chapters of the work. He also never finished *De Vulgari Eloquentia* (On the Eloquence of the Vernacular Tongue), a two-volume discussion of the use of dialects and the merits of Italian as a literary language. Toward the end of his life, he also composed two *Eclogues,* in response to a poetry professor's request that he write in Latin, and wrote *Questio de Aqua et Terra* (Discourse on the Nature of Water and Earth), a scientific essay on the relative levels of water and land on the earth's surface.

Shortly before his death, Dante completed his masterpiece, *La Divina Commedia,* which he had begun in about 1306. *Commedia* (the word "Divina" was added posthumously) has 100 cantos, divided into three nearly equal sections: *Inferno* (Hell), *Purgatorio* (Purgatory), and *Paradiso* (Heaven). The structure of the poem imitates what Dante perceived to be the beauty of God's design, and the allegorical verse, written in a complicated metrical scheme called *terza rima,* describes the poet's pilgrimage—with the guidance of Beatrice, the Roman poet Vergil, and Saint Bernard of Clairvaux—through the afterworld to God. Though Dante led an active, important political life, it is this stirring poetical journey, culminating in the classic *The Inferno,* for which he will always be remembered. Dante is still regarded as the greatest poet of the Italian language and one of the greatest writers in world literature. ❖

Thematic and Structural Analysis

Dante Alighieri's *Inferno* forms the first part of his three-part *Divine Comedy* and records the travels of the character Dante as he journeys through hell, where the souls of the damned suffer for eternity. The second and third parts of the *Divine Comedy* (not covered here), *Purgatorio* and *Paradiso*, describe Dante's travels through purgatory (where, according to medieval Christian thought, the souls of the moderately sinful were punished in order to purify them for heaven) and heaven. In these books, Dante for the most part presents what would have been a familiar picture to his fellow medieval Christians, albeit with some notable idiosyncrasies. While Dante had his disagreements with contemporary religious authorities, he unquestioningly accepted and supported the moral values and claim to divine supremacy of the medieval Christian church.

Canto I of the *Inferno* begins:

> In the middle of the journey of our life I came to myself within a dark wood where the straight way was lost.

This passage holds a multiplicity of meanings that continues throughout the work. First, it begins the tale by placing the starting point of the character Dante's divine journey at a conveniently vague locale. Second, it echoes a common beginning to other stories of conversion and salvation; the sinner, in the "dark wood" of his sin, has lost the "straight way" to God. He has also realized that his ways are in error, a crucial first step in Christian theology to finding salvation. Third, it works on a biographical level: "the middle of the journey of our life" refers to Dante's thirty-fifth year, or the year 1300, more than ten years before the writing of the *Inferno*. Contemporary readers who were informed about local politics would presumably know that 1300 was the year that Dante occupied high office in Florence, Italy, and was shortly before he was driven from office and exiled from Florence. Consequently, the *Inferno* is not simply an imaginative journey, but a journey of religious faith to salvation and an often biting commentary on Italian politics.

As Dante realizes that he is lost in the dark and frightening woods, he sees a hill covered with sunshine. But this is no ordinary mountain: it is "the pass which never yet let any go alive"—the mountain of purgatory, which is bathed in light because of its relative nearness to God. This sign of God's presence both comforts and attracts Dante, but as soon as he begins to climb the mountain, a leopard springs out at him and blocks his way. Dante, realizing that it is the morning of Good Friday and thus an auspicious time, has "good hope of escape" from the leopard, but then a lion and an especially fearsome she-wolf appear and drive Dante back down the hill to the darkness.

Dante (and, according to medieval Christian theology, all sinners) is not going to be able to reach the light without help. But God has not forsaken Dante, who spots a mysterious figure on his way down the hill and pleads with him for assistance. The figure reveals himself to be the spirit of Virgil, a celebrated Latin poet born in 70 B.C.E. whom both the real and the fictional Dante especially revered. Virgil asks Dante why he is fleeing back to the dark forest, and Dante points out the slavering wolf. Virgil tells Dante that he must take another road to God, for the wolf prevents all men from passing. Virgil then makes a prophecy: a hound (possibly Can Grande [Great Dog] della Scala, a lord in Verona who supported Dante after his exile) will slay the wolf and save Italy. In the meantime, Virgil suggests, Dante should follow him through hell and purgatory, eventually reaching heaven (where Virgil, a heathen, may not go). Dante agrees, and the poets set off.

But in **Canto II** Dante is suddenly seized by doubt. After all, he tells Virgil, the only other living people who have journeyed to the afterworld are Aeneas, who founded Rome, and Saint Paul. Dante does not feel that he measures up to these two accomplished men, and he suggests to Virgil that perhaps it is presumptuous of him to make the journey. In order to relieve his fear, Virgil tells Dante how he was sent to help him. Virgil, a heathen (that is, a person who was never introduced to Christianity), lives in limbo, just inside of hell. He was visited by the spirit of a woman "so blessed and so fair that I begged her to command me." She told him of her friend Dante, who she feared had wandered astray and would never reach heaven, where she abides. She then told him her name, Beatrice.

Virgil readily agreed to help her, but then asked her why she left her exalted place in heaven to visit the disgusting confines of hell. She told him that God had rendered her immune to the fires of hell because her mission originated with "a gentle lady in Heaven"—presumably the Virgin Mary, mother of Jesus Christ—who sent Saint Lucy of Syracuse to Beatrice to encourage her to talk to Virgil. Virgil's account of Beatrice's conversation with Lucy emphasizes Beatrice's relationship with Dante while she was still living. The historical identity of Beatrice has been debated by Dante scholars for centuries with no satisfactory resolution, but obviously their relationship while living was sufficiently meaningful to make her become his supernatural protector after death. Virgil's mention of Beatrice emboldens Dante.

Dante's resolution is immediately put to the test in **Canto III**, which opens with the words inscribed on the gates of hell:

THROUGH ME THE WAY INTO THE WOEFUL CITY,
THROUGH ME THE WAY TO THE ETERNAL PAIN,
THROUGH ME THE WAY AMONG THE LOST PEOPLE.
JUSTICE MOVED MY MAKER ON HIGH,
DIVINE POWER MADE ME AND SUPREME WISDOM
    AND PRIMAL LOVE;
BEFORE ME NOTHING WAS CREATED BUT ETERNAL
    THINGS AND I ENDURE ETERNALLY.
ABANDON EVERY HOPE, YE THAT ENTER.

Dante promptly quails but is reassured by Virgil and enters the gate. He hears terrible sighs and moans and asks Virgil who is making such a noise. Virgil replies that these are "the wretched souls of those who lived without disgrace and without praise" mixed with those fallen angels who, during Satan's rebellion, "were not rebels, nor faithful to God, but were for themselves." They are miserable because they are jealous of everybody else's lot. Virgil dismisses them by saying, "Let us not talk of them; but look thou and pass." Dante looks and sees a mass of people chasing after a whirling and impermanent banner, all the while being persecuted by wasps, hornets, and worms. He recognizes several of them, including Pope Celestine V, an elderly hermit (later canonized) who was elected to the papacy by reformers in 1294 but resigned his post after five months at the behest of the man who succeeded him, the notoriously corrupt Pope Boniface VIII.

It is characteristic of Dante's hell that the punishment of the damned is to be what they were in life. Those who were of no account in life remain of no account in death and never recognize the possibility of reform. It is also characteristic of Dante to identify contemporary historical figures well known to his original audience as eternally damned. While this was no doubt motivated in part by spite, it also reflects his intense concern about the corruption and brutality that marked medieval Italian politics, both secular and religious.

Passing the whirling souls, Dante comes to the river Acheron, one of many rivers of the underworld in classical mythology that appear in the *Inferno*. There he sees a throng of damned souls waiting for the ferry across the river. He also meets Charon, a demonic ferryman (also lifted from classical mythology) who recognizes him as living and refuses him passage. Dante has no time to wonder how he will cross, however, because a tremendous earthquake hits, and Dante loses consciousness.

A loud clap of thunder awakens Dante at the beginning of **Canto IV**, and he finds himself on the edge of a deep valley from which cries of pain emerge. Virgil leads him down to the first level of the valley, which is the first circle of hell. (Hell in the *Inferno* is a funnel-shaped cavity that begins just below the surface of the earth.) Here, Dante hears sighs of "grief without torments," and Virgil informs him that this is limbo, home of the virtuous heathen, who live eternally in the hopeless desire of reaching heaven. Dante is immediately curious to know if Virgil witnessed the harrowing of hell, an event that supposedly occurred between Christ's death and his resurrection when his soul went down to hell, gathered together the especially virtuous, and took them up to heaven. Dante carefully words his question because the names of God and Christ cannot be uttered in hell. Virgil recalls the event well, remembering that "a mighty one" came and saved many souls. He reiterates the orthodox Christian version of the harrowing, telling Dante: "And I would have thee know that before these no human souls were saved."

Dante sees a group of heathen set off from the others by a blaze of light. These are four exalted poets (including Virgil) who have God's special favor. There is a fair castle, which contains the souls of a variety of especially virtuous philosophers, moralists, and leaders. But Dante and Virgil must press on, and they descend to the second circle of hell.

There (**Canto V**) they see Minos, the judge of the dead in classical mythology, transformed here into a snarling demon who, after hearing the confession of a soul, "encircles himself with his tail as many times as the grades he will have it [the soul] sent down." Minos initially mistakes Dante for a damned soul, but Virgil corrects him and leads Dante past. They see the souls of the lustful being beaten about by a tremendous windstorm, and Dante calls two souls over to talk with them. They turn out to be a Florentine couple, Francesca da Polenta and Paolo Malatesta, a woman and her husband's brother who were discovered having an affair and were killed by her husband when Dante was seventeen years old. Francesca recounts the sad story, taking some solace in the fact that a deeper circle of hell awaits her husband, and Dante faints with pity.

He regains consciousness in the third circle (**Canto VI**), where a cold rain comes down constantly and Cerberus, the classical three-headed hound of hell, guards the damned. He challenges Virgil and Dante, but Virgil rams dirt down his throats, and Cerberus retires to contemplate his meal. As Virgil and Dante walk through the third circle, a soul recognizes Dante and hails him. The soul is Ciacco, a friend of Dante's from his youth, now damned for gluttony. Dante asks Ciacco to prophesy the future of Florence, which he does with considerable accuracy. These "prophecies"—actually hindsight, since Dante wrote the poem several years after it supposedly takes place—lend verisimilitude to Dante's journey and, more importantly, give Dante an opportunity to pass judgment upon recent events.

After leaving Ciacco, Dante asks what will happen to these souls after the second coming of Christ, and Virgil informs him that they will be reunited with their bodies and then return to their eternal torment, which will be all the more unpleasant. The two proceed to the fourth circle (**Canto VII**), where they are challenged by Plutus, the classical god of wealth. Virgil commands Plutus to let them pass, and they descend to see two groups of souls crashing into each other, only to come apart and crash into each other again. They are those who have been avaricious in life (clerics, according to Virgil, are especially prone to this vice) and those who have been prodigal. Dante attempts to recognize some, but they are too disfigured by their sin. Virgil continues in his role of explicator of the universe by telling Dante that Fortune is one of God's "primal creatures" who watches over and guides a certain part of the universe according to wisdom and rules that are divine and good but also incomprehensible to human beings.

Descending to the fifth circle, Dante and Virgil come upon the Styx, a marsh. Dante sees that it is full of people who are attacking one another; Virgil reveals that these souls were ruled by anger while alive, while those who were constantly sullen are now stuck in the bottom of the mire. As **Canto VIII** opens, the two pass through the marsh and Dante sees a tower that is sending out signals with a light. The two are intercepted by a boat rowed by Phlegyas, a character from classical mythology who, while enraged, had once burned down a temple of Apollo, the sun god. Phlegyas first thinks that he has found two damned souls and is characteristically furious when he discovers his mistake. (Dante's devils usually suffer from the same personality flaws as the damned souls they punish.) Dante and Virgil board the boat, and Phlegyas rows them to the tower.

As they travel through the marsh, a spirit rises from the mud and claims to know Dante. Dante recognizes him as Filippo Argenti, a wealthy nobleman of Florence who had fueled division and violence in the city, and he takes great pleasure at seeing him attacked by his fellows. Although Dante's enjoyment may strike the reader as distasteful, the sowing of political division in medieval Italy was no minor sin, since it generally led to murder and warfare. In addition, the character of Dante, by seeing the justice of such punishment rather than feeling pity, is beginning to understand and accept the higher wisdom of God in creating such a place as hell.

Dante and Virgil leave the marsh and reach the gates of the city of Dis, which is the gateway to the "nether Hell." But the devils of Dis refuse them entrance, defying Virgil and sending the hideous Gorgons to molest them (**Canto IX**). Dante is frightened, but soon a large and powerful angel strides down from heaven, opens the gates, warns the devils not to interfere, and strides away. Dante and Virgil enter the sixth circle of hell to discover a large, burning graveyard that contains the souls of the heretics.

As they pass through the yard (**Canto X**), a voice booms from one of the sepulchers, claiming Dante as a fellow country-man. Dante turns to meet Farinata degli Uberti, a leader of the Ghibellines, a Florentine family that fought the Guelfs, the faction to which Dante's family belongs. Although Farinata helped massacre the Guelfs in 1260, he and Dante address one another with respect. Further undercutting the families' division, Farinata shares his tomb with his Guelf counterpart, Cavalcante.

As Dante and Virgil leave the graveyard, the stench becomes especially offensive (**Canto XI**). Virgil suggests that they sit by the fiery tomb of Pope Anastasius (a fifth-century pope who denied the divine birth of Christ) while he explains the layout of hell to Dante. The seventh circle of hell, Virgil says, contains the violent, subdivided into those who have committed violence against others, against themselves (suicides), and against God (blasphemers) and God's creation, nature (sodomites and usurers). The fraudulent occupy the eight and ninth circles of hell. The simply fraudulent of the eighth circle include hypocrites, corrupt civil and religious officials, flatterers, thieves, pimps, seducers, and sorcerers. But the ninth circle is reserved for the treacherous—those who have defrauded those to whom they have a special responsibility. Dante asks why all sinners do not live within the walls of Dis, and Virgil explains that Dis divides those who have sinned simply by allowing their passions to get the better of them from the violent and the fraudulent, who have behaved in a malicious and calculated fashion.

On that note, Virgil and Dante head to the border between the sixth and seventh circles of hell (**Canto XII**). There they discover the steep remains of a major landslide and see the Minotaur, whom they flee by descending the slope. Virgil, who visited these parts before the crucifixion of Christ, remarks that the slope was whole before, but that there was a large earthquake a few days before the harrowing of hell, which may have been responsible for the landslide. Virgil does not know why the earthquake happened, but Dante surely means to bring to mind to the reader that, according to the Bible, when Christ was crucified a tremendous earthquake struck, obviously affecting the underworld as well. With his uninformed intuition, Virgil falls back on another heathen philosopher, Empedocles, and attributes the earthquake to the fact that "the universe felt love."

The pair runs into a group of centaurs who watch over the souls of the seventh circle. The souls themselves stand forever in a moat of boiling blood (later revealed to be the river Phlegethon). In **Canto XIII** the two cross the moat at a ford and enter a wood where Harpies live. Virgil encourages Dante to break a twig off a tree; when he does so, the tree bleeds and speaks to him, revealing itself and all the other trees to be the souls of suicides. The tree (actually the soul of Piero delle Vigne, a royal advisor who killed himself in 1249) tells Dante that the Harpies constantly tear him. When the second coming arrives, reveals Piero, those who destroyed their own bodies will not be allowed to reoccupy them but will instead hang their bodies from their limbs. In the midst of their conversation, a chase is heard, and two notorious thirteenth-century spend-thrifts, Lano of Siena and Giacomo of Padua, run onto the scene. Lano outruns Giacomo, who is torn to bits by their pursuers, a pack of black hounds. The chase (which implies that spendthrifts are also violent against themselves) damages a neighboring bush, which turns out to be the soul of a Florentine who hanged himself in his house.

Leaving the wood, Dante and Virgil come upon the violent against God and nature (**Canto XIV**), who inhabit a dreadful desert where fire rains down upon them. A few of these souls are lying down, making them the most exposed to the fire; these are revealed to be the blasphemers, and one of them, Capaneus, aptly demonstrates his useless defiance of God. Virgil leads Dante to a stream with paved banks that leads through the desert, and Dante observes that the fire does not rain down on the banks. Virgil takes a moment to explain that all the rivers of the afterworld have a common source, namely a mysterious old man who lives in a mountain on the isle of Crete where Jupiter, the classical god of thunder, was raised. The man's body is made up of different substances that reflect the different ages of humanity, from the glorious golden age of the past to the considerably less glorious present day. His head is gold, his upper body silver, his lower torso brass, his legs iron, and his right foot clay. His body (except for his golden head) is split (representing the imperfection of humanity), and from this fissure drop tears, which are the source of all the rivers in the afterworld.

In **Canto XV** Dante and Virgil proceed down the banks of the river, passing alongside groups of walking souls, when one recognizes Dante. He is Brunetto Latini, an older admired Florentine statesman, and he walks alongside Dante, discussing current and future events. In **Canto XVI** Dante then encounters three other sodomites, all, like Latini, well-respected Guelfs of an earlier generation. They are especially eager to talk to him because he can make certain that they are remembered in the world of the living. They all bemoan Florence's current state of moral decline. The Florentines leave, and Dante and Virgil reach the edge of the seventh circle, which is a high cliff. Dante hands Virgil a rope he has tied around his waist, and Virgil throws it into the abyss.

In response, a hideous monster, Geryon, crawls out of the abyss (**Canto XVII**). An emblem of hypocrisy, Geryon has the face of a kind man, a serpent's body, two hairy arms, and a large scorpion's tail with a poisonous sting. Virgil directs Dante to where the monster is waiting, then changes his mind and sends Dante to speak with some usurers. They are quite unfriendly, and after identifying them, Dante returns to the monster to discover that Virgil is already on its back. Dante climbs aboard, frightened but relieved to have Virgil near, and Geryon descends to the eighth circle.

The eighth circle (**Canto XVIII**) is called Malebolge, or Evil Pouches, and is a series of ten circular canyons nested inside each other. A series of ridges crosses the canyons like spokes on a wheel, passing over the canyons as bridges. The entire eighth circle slants down to the middle, where passage to the ninth circle can be found. Malebolge is home to the simply fraudulent, and in the first canyon Dante sees Venedico Caccianemico, a contemporary of Dante's who reportedly sold his sister's sexual favors, and Jason, a figure from classical legend who was a great seducer. Both pimps and seducers are being run and whipped by demons. In the next canyon, Dante sees the flatterers, who are forced to stand in human excrement.

The third canyon (**Canto XIX**) holds the corrupt clergymen, who lie head down in special nooks while their feet are consumed by flame. Dante enters the canyon to speak to one whose feet burn with a redder flame than the others; the sinner turns out to be none other than Pope Nicholas II, who died in 1280. Nicholas not only mistakes Dante for Pope Boniface VIII, who he knows will join him soon (Boniface died in 1303), but claims that both their corruptions will be overshadowed by that of Pope Clementine V, who was elected in 1305. Dante and Virgil leave the pope and continue to the fourth canyon (**Canto XX**), where diviners and sorcerers walk, their bodies hideously distorted so that they can only see behind them. Virgil takes a moment to point out the sorceress Manto and to correct his own account in the *Aeneid* of the founding of his hometown, Mantua, which was named after her. In his original account, Virgil said that Manto founded the city; in this "corrected" version, Virgil (reflecting the author's distaste for magicians) claims that she merely died where the city was eventually built.

The two continue inward and downward to the fifth canyon (**Canto XXI**), which is filled with boiling tar. They spot a group of devils tossing a soul into the tar and pushing him below the surface with long hooked gaffs; the devils reveal that this is the place where the souls of corrupt government officials are punished. Virgil confronts the devils, who agree to let the two pass but point out that the earthquake destroyed the bridge across the sixth canyon formed by the ridge on which they are walking. In **Canto XXII** Virgil and Dante agree to follow the devils around to the next ridge. While walking, the devils spot a tormented soul popping out of the tar to cool off and grab him with their hooks. They mangle him, but he manages to tell Dante and Virgil that although he is French there are a number of prominent Italians under the tar with him. The soul then tells the assembled devils that he will call some of the other souls out of the tar; eager to torture the others and sure they can catch the one if he tries to go back under, they release him. He is too quick for them, however, and ducks back into the tar. Two of the devils start fighting, and they fall into the tar as Dante and Virgil judiciously exit the scene.

In **Canto XXIII** the devils pursue the two but are unable by divine ordinance to enter the sixth canyon, where Dante and

Virgil discover the souls of the hypocrites. These souls are doomed to walk the course of the canyon wearing cloaks that are beautifully gilded on the outside but lined with a heavy weight of lead on the inside. Dante speaks with one who is a member of the Knights of Saint Mary, called the Jovial Friars, a religious order founded in 1260 ostensibly for the protection of the weak. Dante also spots a man staked to the ground as if crucified so that all the hypocrites step on him as they walk through the canyon. The Jovial Friar tells Dante that this is Caiaphas, who counseled the Jews to allow Christ to be crucified, and that his father-in-law, Annas, is staked in a similar fashion on the far side of the canyon for the same offense. Virgil is astounded by Caiaphas, who was not there when he came before and whose offense he as a heathen cannot comprehend. The limits to Virgil's abilities are made still more evident when the Jovial Friar reveals that all the bridges across the sixth canyon have collapsed and that Virgil had been misled by the devils of the fifth.

Virgil and Dante labor up the wall of the sixth canyon and, unable to see into the seventh, enter it. There (**Canto XXIV**) they find a group of naked souls running about plagued by a tremendous number of snakes. These are the souls of thieves, and when one passing Dante and Virgil is bitten by a snake, he quickly burns up, then just as quickly appears whole again. Dante asks him who he is, and he says he is Vanni Fucci, who stole holy objects from a church, a crime that remained concealed until after his death. Fucci is so ashamed to reveal his sin that he lashes out at Dante and then curses God (**Canto XXV**), but a serpent encircles his neck to choke off further blasphemy and a centaur pursues him. Dante and Virgil witness more strange interactions between the thieves and the snakes: One snake merges his body with that of a thief; another turns a human soul into a snake while changing himself into a human.

Dante and Virgil proceed to the eighth canyon (**Canto XXVI**), where they find the souls of false counselors being consumed in ever-burning bright flame. One turns out to be Ulysses; when asked by Virgil about his death, he recounts that he left home for one last adventure and, like Dante at the beginning of the poem, saw the mountain of purgatory. Unlike Dante, he did not seek divine assistance in reaching the light and perished. When Ulysses finishes, another flame speaks, asking for news of Italy (**Canto XXVII**). Dante recounts current events and asks the flame its story. Unlike the other souls, this flame does not want his tale told to the living; he is Guido da Montefeltro, a military leader who became a Franciscan monk later in life. Asked to advise Pope Boniface VIII as to the best way to conquer a city, Montefeltro had come up with an idea: the pope could pretend to make peace with its inhabitants, then break his trust and slaughter them. At first, he was reluctant to share this unethical plan with the pope, but Boniface promised to absolve him of the sin. However, when Montefeltro died and Saint Francis came to take his soul to heaven, a devil pointed out that "he cannot be absolved who repents not" and hauled him down to hell.

Dante and Virgil proceed to the ninth canyon (**Canto XXVIII**), where people who cause division within the church or state are punished by having their bodies divided, i.e., dismembered or cut open. Among them are the prophet of Islam, Mahomet, and a member of Dante's family, Geri del Bello, who caused discord in another family. Entering the tenth and final canyon (**Cantos XXIX–XXX**), Dante and Virgil see souls plagued with a variety of diseases, including skin disorders and dropsy (uncontrolled swelling). These are the souls of people who impersonated others or who counterfeited coins. Dante speaks with a number of them and witnesses a nasty argument between a counterfeiter and an impersonator before Virgil takes him away, chiding him for enjoying the quarrel.

Dante's shame is such that he is quickly forgiven, and the two continue on their journey, reaching the inside edge of the eighth circle of hell (**Canto XXXI**), where monstrous giants are trapped, buried up to their waists in the ground. Virgil importunes one to pick them up and move them to the ninth circle, where the treacherous are punished (**Canto XXXII**). The ninth circle is divided into four sections: Caina, for the treacherous to kindred; Antenora, for the treacherous to country or cause; Ptolomea, for the treacherous to guests; and Judecca, for the treacherous to lords and benefactors.

When Dante is set down in Caina, he is surprised to realize that the ground beneath his feet is the ice of the river Cocytus and souls are frozen in it up to their necks. Although immobile, the souls of Caina are frozen so that their faces are down and they can avoid recognition. When Dante asks a pair who are frozen next to each other to identify themselves, they refuse to answer, but another soul, displaying his treacherous nature, names them and just about everyone else in sight. Dante continues on, reaching Antenora where the souls' faces are pointed forward, and accidentally trips over one of them. The soul mentions that he was in part responsible for the rout of the Guelfs by the Ghibellines in 1260, and Dante tries to discover his name. Fearful of further shame, the soul refuses to tell Dante, but a neighboring traitor proves helpful and tells Dante that this is Bocca; Bocca naturally returns the favor, revealing the other's identity as well as that of all the other occupants of Antenora that he knows.

Dante and Virgil leave Bocca only to come upon a dreadful sight in **Canto XXXIII**. Two souls are frozen together, one behind the other, and the soul in back is biting and chewing the head of the soul in front. The one in back speaks to Dante and Virgil, telling them that he is Count Ugolino of Pisa and his victim is the Archbishop Ruggieri. In the 1280s, Ugolino held a position of authority in Pisa, a position he maintained through treachery. But in 1289, Ruggieri, a former conspirator, turned against him and locked Ugolino and his offspring (actually two grown sons and two grandsons, but described in the poem as four young sons) in a jail and let them starve to death. Ugolino describes his ordeal in heart-wrenching terms (and conveniently excludes his reasons for being damned), but while his tale is tragic, he himself is flawed. At no point in his ordeal was he able to rise above his misery and hatred, and as a damned soul transcendence has become impossible.

Dante and Virgil continue to Ptolomea, where the souls are frozen so that their faces are uplifted and their tears freeze over their eyes, blinding them. Dante feels a breeze and asks Virgil its cause, but Virgil tells him he will find out soon enough. A soul, hearing them speak, cries out to them to remove his frozen mask of tears. Dante asks him who he is, cunningly promising to go down to the bottom of the ice (where he is headed anyway) if he does not help the soul in return. The soul reveals himself to be the infamous Fra Alberigo, who invited his younger brother and his son to a banquet and murdered them.

Dante exclaims that he thought Alberigo was still alive, and Alberigo reveals that when a truly dire sin is committed, the soul goes immediately to hell, while the body, appearing to live on, is actually possessed by a devil. Dante—after determining that the Genoan Branca D'Oria, who killed his father-in-law at a banquet in 1290 and is still apparently living, is in fact in hell—leaves Alberigo without clearing his eyes, claiming "it was courtesy to be a churl to him."

In **Canto XXXIV** Dante and Virgil enter Judecca, where the souls are frozen completely in the ice, and a large, windmill-like object can be seen ahead. As they get closer, Virgil tells Dante that the object is Satan, who is unbelievably large and ugly. The wind that blows through the ninth circle comes from Satan's three pairs of batlike wings; these not only freeze the souls into the ice but freeze Satan as well. He has three faces, one red, one pale yellow, and one black. Tears of bloody foam drip from his eyes, and in his three mouths he mangles three souls. Virgil identifies them as Judas Iscariot, who betrayed Christ (the embodiment of true religion), and Brutus and Cassius, who betrayed Julius Caesar (the embodiment of just rule).

Virgil commands Dante to grab him around the neck, and then he approaches Satan, grabs his hairy leg, and climbs downward. Halfway down the leg, Virgil turns around, and a panicky Dante thinks they must be returning to hell. Virgil passes through a cleft in a rock and puts Dante down, and Dante, looking up through the cleft, sees that he is under Satan's feet. Dante becomes even more confused when Virgil tells him that it is now Saturday morning; when they approached Satan, it was Saturday night. Virgil reveals that they have passed through the center of the earth, which is located directly under Jerusalem (where Christ was crucified) and which is also the center of gravity. Virgil turned while climbing down Satan's leg to compensate for the gravitational shift, and they gained twelve hours because they are now in the opposite hemisphere. Both the chasm of hell and the mountain of purgatory were formed when Satan was expelled from heaven and fell from the sky. Dante is satisfied with and enlightened by these explanations, and the *Inferno* ends with him obediently following Virgil on the climb into purgatory. ✤

—*Mary Sisson*

List of Characters

Dante (Dante Alighieri), a deeply religious fourteenth-century Italian poet and politician, is both the author of the poem and its protagonist. The poem takes place in 1300, just as Dante's career in Florentine politics is taking a downward turn that will result in his exile. Dante journeys through hell in the *Inferno;* in the process he learns about the nature of the universe and his own special role in it.

Virgil, Dante's guide through hell, is a Latin poet from Mantua born in 70 B.C.E. and the author of the *Aeneid,* an epic poem about the founding of Rome. Like Dante, Virgil is both a historical person and a fictional character within the poem. Virgil is a heathen who lived without the knowledge of Christ; as a result, in the universe of the *Divine Comedy* he has no hope of salvation, and although he is very knowledgeable, his wisdom is inherently imperfect.

Beatrice is a woman whom Dante once loved and who has since died. Beatrice's exact historical identity remains unknown, but in the poem she occupies an exalted position in heaven. She has a small but crucial role in the *Inferno,* where she acts as a supernatural protector for Dante.

Farinata degli Uberti is one of many Italian political figures Dante comes across in hell. Farinata led the Ghibelline faction to defeat the Guelf faction in 1260. Dante's family is Guelf, but he finds Farinata (who is burning as a heretic) to be an admirable character.

Pope Nicolas II is one of many religious leaders whom Dante meets in hell. Nicolas's feet are licked by flames as punishment for being a corrupt clergyman who bought his office and whose favor could be bought as well. Nicolas embodies Dante's opinion of the popes of his day, who he felt had betrayed the church with their ambition for worldly things.

Ulysses, the hero of Homer's *Odyssey,* is engulfed in flames in Dante's hell for being a false counselor. Ulysses embodies the failure of humans to attain salvation without the knowledge of Christ; when he attempts to enter purgatory as a living man, he is killed and damned.

Count Ugolino of Pisa is a corrupt Pisan politician who was locked in a cell with his children by Archbishop Ruggieri and allowed to starve (critics disagree on whether or not he was forced by hunger to eat their flesh). Ugolino spends eternity frozen in ice, gnawing the head of the archbishop.

Satan, also called Lucifer, Dis (the name of the city separating upper hell from lower hell), and a variety of other names, is the lord of hell, formerly an angel who turned against God and was expelled from heaven. Like the other devils, Satan occupies a level of hell appropriate to his crime. His means of punishing others (beating his wings so that the sinners are frozen in ice) also punishes him (he is frozen in the ice as well). ✤

Above translations are John D. Sinclair's.

Critical Views

DANTE ON THE NATURE AND PURPOSE OF *THE DIVINE COMEDY*

[Dante's most significant statement on the nature and purpose of his poem occurs in a letter to Can Grande della Scala, written probably in 1319. Here, Dante notes that his work must be interpreted both literally and allegorically, and he supplies an explanation of his use of the word "comedy."]

If any one ⟨. . .⟩ is desirous of offering any sort of introduction to part of a work, it behoves him to furnish some notion of the whole of which it is a part. Wherefore I, too, being desirous of offering something by way of introduction to the above-mentioned part of the whole *Comedy,* thought it incumbent on me in the first place to say something concerning the work as a whole, in order that access to the part might be the easier and the more perfect. There are six points, then, as to which inquiry must be made at the beginning of every didactic work; namely, the subject, the author, the form, the aim, the title of the book, and the branch of philosophy to which it belongs. Now of these six points there are three in respect of which the part which I have had in mind to address to you differs from the whole work; namely, the subject, the form, and the title; whereas in respect of the others there is no difference, as is obvious to any one who considers the matter. Consequently, in an examination of the whole, these three points must be made the subject of a separate inquiry; which being done, the way will be sufficiently clear for the introduction to the part. Later we will examine the other three points, not only with reference to the whole work, but also with reference to the particular part which is offered to you.

For the elucidation therefore, of what we have to say, it must be understood that the meaning of this work is not of one kind only; rather the work may be described as 'polysemous', that is, having several meanings; for the first meaning is that which is conveyed by the letter, and the next is that which is conveyed by what the letter signifies; the former of which is called literal, while the latter is called allegorical, or mystical. And for the better illustration of this method of exposition we may apply it to the following verses: 'When Israel went out of Egypt, the house of Jacob from a people of strange language; Judah was his sanctuary, and Israel his dominion'. For if we consider the letter alone, the thing signified to us is the going out of the children of Israel from Egypt in the time of Moses; if the allegory, our redemption through Christ is signified; if the moral sense, the conversion of the soul from the sorrow and misery of sin to a state of grace is signified: if the anagogical, the passing of the sanctified soul from the bondage of the corruption of this world to the liberty of everlasting glory is signified. And although these mystical meanings are called by various names, they may one and all in a general sense be termed allegorical, inasmuch as they are different (*diversi*) from the literal or historical; for the word 'allegory' is so called from the Greek *alleon,* which in Latin is *alienum* (strange) or *diversum* (different).

This being understood, it is clear that the subject, with regard to which the alternative meanings are brought into play, must be twofold. And therefore the subject of this work must be considered in the first place from the point of view of the literal meaning, and next from that of the allegorical interpretation. The subject, then, of the whole work, taken in the literal sense only, is the state of souls after death, pure and simple. For on and about that the argument of the whole work turns. If, however, the work be regarded from the allegorical point of view, the subject is man according as by his merits or demerits in the exercise of his free will he is deserving of reward or punishment by justice.

And the form is twofold—the form of the treatise, and the form of the treatment. The form of the treatise is threefold, according to the threefold division. The first division is that whereby the whole work is divided into three cantiche; the second, whereby each cantica is divided into cantos; and the third, whereby each canto is divided into rhymed lines. The form or manner of treatment is poetic, fictive, descriptive, digressive, and figurative; and further, it is definitive, analytical, probative, refutative, and exemplificative.

The title of the book is 'Here begins the *Comedy* of Dante Alighieri, a Florentine by birth, not by disposition'. For the understanding of which it must be noted that 'comedy' is so called from *comos*, a village, and *oda*, a song; whence comedy is as it were a 'rustic song'. Now comedy is a certain kind of poetical narration which differs from all others. It differs, then, from tragedy in its subject-matter, in that tragedy at the beginning is admirable and placid, but at the end or issue is foul and horrible. And tragedy is so called from *tragos*, a goat, and *oda;* as it were a 'goat-song', that is to say foul like a goat, as appears from the tragedies of Seneca. Whereas comedy begins with sundry adverse conditions, but ends happily, as appears from the comedies of Terence. And for this reason it is the custom of some writers in their salutation to say by way of greeting: 'a tragic beginning and a comic ending to you!' Tragedy and comedy differ likewise in their style of language; for that of tragedy is high-flown and sublime, while that of comedy is unstudied and lowly. And this is implied by Horace in the *Art of Poetry,* where he grants that the comedian may on occasion use the language of tragedy, and vice versa:

> Yet sometimes comedy her voice will raise,
> And angry Chremes scold with swelling phrase;
> And prosy periods oft our ears assail
> When Telephus and Peleus tell their tragic tale.

And from this it is clear that the present work is to be described as a comedy. For if we consider the subject matter, at the beginning it is horrible and foul, as being *Hell;* but at the close it is happy, desirable, and pleasing, as being *Paradise.* As regards the style of language, the style is unstudied and lowly, as being in the vulgar tongue, in which even women-folk hold their talk. And hence it is evident why the work is called a comedy.

—Dante Alighieri, Letter to Can Grande della Scala (c. 1319), *The Letters of Dante,* ed. and tr. Paget Toynbee (Oxford: Clarendon Press, 1920), pp. 198–201

[Giambattista Vico (1668–1744) was a pioneering philosopher and historian whose major work, *Scienza nuova* (The New Science), propounded his view of historical change as a recurrent cycle between barbarism and civilization. In this extract from an essay on Dante, Vico states that Dante's poem is to be read from three perspectives.]

Dante Alighieri's *Commedia* should be read from a triple perspective: as a history of the barbarous times of Italy, as a source of beautiful Tuscan sayings, and as an example of sublime poetry.

As far as the first one is concerned, it is ordered and set out by nature in this way: poets sing of true stories at the time when, within a certain uniformity in the course taken by their common spirit, nations begin to refine their own barbarousness—which is naturally open and truthful because it lacks reflection that, applied to evil, is the only mother of falsehood. So in the *New Science around the Nature of Nations,* we have professed Homer to be the first historian of gentility; this is confirmed in the *Annotations* that we wrote to that work, in which we have found Homer to be entirely different from what the world has hitherto believed him to be. And certainly the first historian of the Romans known to us was Ennius, who sang of the Carthaginian wars. In the same manner, Dante was the first Italian historian, or one among the first. What he mixed as a poet in his *Commedia* is the narration of the dead who reside, according to the merits of each, in hell, in purgatory, or in paradise. And here, as a poet, he must "sic veris falsa remiscet" in order to be like Homer or Ennius—conforming, however, to our Christian religion, which teaches us that the rewards and the punishments of our good as well as of our evil actions are eternal rather than temporal. Thus, the allegories of this poem are no more than those reflections that the reader of history must make by himself so as to profit from the examples of others.

Second, Dante should be read as a pure and vast source of beautiful Tuscan sayings. In this area he has not yet obtained a profitable commentary, and this is why it is commonly said that Dante has gathered the sayings of all the dialects of Italy. This false opinion can only be due to one thing: during the sixteenth century (cinquecento), learned men began to cultivate the Tuscan tongue, which was spoken in Florence in the fourteenth century—the golden century of this language. They noticed in Dante a great number of sayings that were not to be found in other Tuscan writers; since they realized by chance that some of them were still alive in the tongues of other Italian peoples, they believed that Dante had gathered them and brought them together in his *Commedia*. The same fate befell Homer: almost all of the peoples of Greece claimed him as their citizen, for each people recognized in his poems its own native and living sayings. But such an opinion is false for two very serious reasons. First of all, in those times Florence must have had the majority of the sayings shared by all the other cities of Italy; otherwise the Italian tongue would not have been the same as the Florentine tongue. The second reason is that, in those unhappy centuries, there were no writers in the vulgar tongue in the other cities of Italy, as in fact none has come down to us. Therefore, Dante's own life would not have sufficed to learn the vulgar tongues from so many peoples so as to have available, during the composition of his *Commedia*, all those sayings that he needed in order to explain himself. Hence it would be necessary for the Academics of the Crusca to send throughout Italy a catalog of such words and sayings, especially among the lower orders of the city, who preserve the ancient customs and languages better than the noblemen and the men of the courts, and then among the peasants, who actually preserve even better than the lower orders of the cities such customs and languages. Thus, the Academics would be informed about how many and which ones of these are used and in what way, and they would thus gain a true understanding.

Third, Dante should be read in order to contemplate a rare example of a sublime poet. For this is the nature of sublime poetry: it does not let itself be learned by any artifice. Homer is the most sublime poet among all those who came after him, nor did he have a Longinus before him who could have given him some precepts of poetic sublimity. And even the principal sources shown by Longinus can only be enjoyed by those on whom it was bestowed and fated by the Heavens. The most sacred and the most profound of these are only two: first, a loftiness of the spirit, which cares only for glory and immortality and despises and disdains all that is admired by avaricious, ambitious, loose, and delicate men of effeminate habits; second, a spirit infused with great public virtues, above all, magnanimity and justice. The Spartans, for example, were forbidden by the law to be literate. However, without any artifice and thanks to the sublime education of their children imposed on them by Lycurgus, every day they used commonly such great and sublime expressions that the most famous heroic and tragic poets would do well to use similar ones in their own poems. But the greatest value of Dante's sublimity lies in the birth of his great mind during the times of the dying barbarousness of Italy. Because human minds are like plots of land: after being uncultivated for long centuries they are finally put to cultivation, and if at first they yield marvelously perfect, large, and copious fruit, they are soon tired of being more and more cultivated, and they yield few, tasteless, and small fruit. This is the reason that, at the end of the barbarous times, there came Dante for sublime poetry, Petrarch for delicate poetry, and Boccaccio for exquisite and graceful prose. All three are incomparable examples, which must in all cases be followed but which can in no way be attained. But in our most cultured times, some beautiful works of the mind are being crafted, in which others may erect themselves in the hope not only of attaining them but of actually surpassing them.

The anonymous author, I believe, took all this into consideration when he wrote his *Annotations to Dante's "Commedia."* In these, through a rare mixture of clarity and brevity, he makes probable the story of the things, events, and people mentioned by the poet, and he explains his feelings with reasonableness. It thus becomes possible to understand the beauty as well as the gracefulness of his sayings, their ornament as well as their loftiness. (This, in fact, is the most efficient way of attaining the language of good writers: to enter into the spirit of what they felt and of what they intended to say. And it is in this way that, in the cinquecento, so many very famous writers succeeded, both in prose and in verse, even before the celebration of the Calepini and of many other dictionaries.) The author of the

Annotations omits every moral and any other erudite allegory, nor does he pontificate about poetic art; rather, he makes an effort so that youth may read him with that pleasure savored by human minds—a pleasure thanks to which, without the danger or being disgusted, they shortly learn much from long commentaries, to which commentators usually reduce with uneasiness all that they comment. Therefore I consider them most useful especially during these times, in which we want to know the essence of things with clarity and ease.

—Giambattista Vico, "Discoverta del vero Dante ovvero nuovi principi di critica dantesca" (1728–29), *Critical Essays on Dante,* ed. Giuseppe Mazzotta (Boston: G. K. Hall, 1991), pp. 58–60 (tr. Cristina M. Mazzoni)

THOMAS WARTON ON THE INELEGANCIES OF DANTE'S DESCRIPTIONS

[Thomas Warton (1728–1790) was a poet who is today best known for an important critical study, *The History of English Poetry* (1774–81). In an extract from that work, Warton, in comparing Dante to Milton, finds many of Dante's powerful descriptions of hell to be inelegant and distasteful.]

Antaeus, whose body stands ten ells high from the pit, is commanded by Virgil to advance. They both mount on his shoulders, and are thus carried about Cocytus. The giant, says the poet, moved off with us like the mast of a ship. One cannot help observing what has been indeed already hinted, how judiciously Milton, in a similar argument, has retained the just beauties, and avoided the childish or ludicrous excesses of these bold inventions. At the same time we may remark, how Dante has sometimes heightened, and sometimes diminished by improper additions or misrepresentations, the legitimate descriptions of Virgil.

One of the torments of the Damned in Dante's *Inferno,* is the punishment of being eternally confined in lakes of ice.

> Eran l' ombre dolenti nell ghiaccia,
> Mettendo i denti in nota di cicogna.

The ice is described to be like that of the Danube or Tanais. This species of infernal torment, which is neither directly warranted by scripture, nor suggested in the systems of the Platonic fabulists, and which has been adopted both by Shakespeare and Milton, has its origin in the legendary hell of the monks. The hint seems to have been taken from an obscure text in the Book of *Job*, dilated by Saint Jerom, and the early commentators. The torments of hell, in which the punishment by cold is painted at large, had formed a visionary romance, under the name of Saint Patrick's Purgatory or Cave, long before Dante wrote. The venerable Bede, who lived in the seventh century, has framed a future mansion of existence for departed souls with this mode of torture. In the hands of Dante it has assumed many fantastic and grotesque circumstances, which make us laugh and shudder at the same time.

In another department, Dante represents some of his criminals rolling themselves in human ordure. If his subject led him to such a description, he might at least have used decent expressions. But his diction is not here less sordid than his imagery. I am almost afraid to transcribe this gross passage, even in the disguise of the old Tuscan phraseology.

> quindi giù nel fosso
> vidi gente atuffata in uno sterco
> che da gli uman privati para mosso.
> Et mentre che làggiù con l'occhio cerco,
> vidi un co' capo si da merda lordo,
> che non *parea s' era laico, o cherco*

The humour of the last line does not make amends for the nastiness of the image. It is not to be supposed, that a man of strong sense and genius, whose understanding had been cultivated by a most exact education, and who had passed his life in the courts of sovereign princes, would have indulged himself in these disgusting fooleries, had he been at all apprehensive that his readers would have been disgusted. But rude and early poets describe everything. They follow the public manners: and if they are either obscene or indelicate, it should be remembered that they wrote before obscenity or indelicacy became offensive.

—Thomas Warton, *The History of English Poetry* (London: Dodsley, 1774–81), Vol. 3, pp. 247–49

WILLIAM HAZLITT ON DANTE'S PLACE IN HISTORY

[William Hazlitt (1778–1830) was one of the leading British literary critics of his age. Among his many works are *Characters of Shakespear's Plays* (1817), *Lectures on the English Comic Writers* (1819), and *Lectures on the English Poets* (1818), from which the following extract is taken. Here, Hazlitt sees Dante as the first poet to emerge from the "barbarism" of the Middle Ages.]

Dante was the father of modern poetry, and he may therefore claim a place in this connection. His poem is the first great step from Gothic darkness and barbarism; and the struggle of thought in it to burst the thraldom in which the human mind had been so long held, is felt in every page. He stood bewildered, not appalled, on that dark shore which separates the ancient and the modern world; and saw the glories of antiquity dawning through the abyss of time, while revelation opened its passage to the other world. He was lost in wonder at what had been done before him, and he dared to emulate it. Dante seems to have been indebted to the Bible for the gloomy tone of his mind, as well as for the prophetic fury which exalts and kindles his poetry; but he is utterly unlike Homer. His genius is not a sparkling flame, but the sullen heat of a furnace. He is power, passion, self-will personified. In all that relates to the descriptive or fanciful part of poetry, he bears no comparison to many who had gone before, or who have come after him; but there is a gloomy abstraction in his conceptions, which lies like a dead weight upon the mind; a benumbing stupor, a breathless awe, from the intensity of the impression; a terrible obscurity, like that which oppresses us in dreams; an identity of interest, which moulds every object to its own purposes, and clothes all things with the passions and imaginations of the human soul,—that make amends for all other deficiencies. The immediate objects he presents to the mind are not much in themselves, they want grandeur, beauty, and order; but they become every thing by the force of the character he impresses upon them. His mind lends its own power to the objects which it contemplates, instead of borrowing it from them. He takes advantage even of the nakedness and dreary vacuity of his subject. His imagination peoples the shades of death, and broods over the silent air. He is the severest of all writers, the most hard and impenetrable, the most opposite to the flowery and glittering; who relies most on his own power, and the sense of it in others, and who leaves most room to the imagination of his readers. Dante's only endeavour is to interest; and he interests by exciting our sympathy with the emotion by which he is himself possessed. He does not place before us the objects by which that emotion has been created; but he seizes on the attention, by shewing us the effect they produce on his feelings; and his poetry accordingly gives the same thrilling and overwhelming sensation, which is caught by gazing on the face of a person who has seen some object of horror. The improbability of the events, the abruptness and monotony in the Inferno, are excessive: but the interest never flags, from the continued earnestness of the author's mind. Dante's great power is in combining internal feelings with external objects. Thus the gate of hell, on which that withering inscription is written, seems to be endowed with speech and consciousness, and to utter its dread warning, not without a sense of mortal woes. This author habitually unites the absolutely local and individual with the greatest wildness and mysticism. In the midst of the obscure and shadowy regions of the lower world, a tomb suddenly rises up with the inscription, 'I am the tomb of Pope Anastasius the Sixth', and half the personages whom he has crowded into the Inferno are his own acquaintance. All this, perhaps, tends to heighten the effect by the bold intermixture of realities, and by an appeal, as it were, to the individual knowledge and experience of the reader. He affords few subjects for picture. There is, indeed, one gigantic one, that of

Count Ugolino, of which Michael Angelo made a bas-relief, and which Sir Joshua Reynolds ought not to have painted.

—William Hazlitt, *Lectures on the English Poets* (1818), *The Complete Works of William Hazlitt*, ed. P. P. Howe (London: J. M. Dent, 1930), Vol. 5, pp. 17–18

Epiphanius Wilson on Dante, Vergil, and Homer

[Epiphanius Wilson (1845–1916) was a prominent literary scholar and Orientalist. He is the author of *Oriental Literature* (1900), *Arabian Literature* (1902), and *Hindu Literature* (1902). In the following extract from his book on Dante, Wilson contrasts Dante's epic with the classical epics of Homer and Vergil, saying that Dante is concerned with the destiny of humanity, whereas the classical poets are concerned with the forces of nature.]

Dante is the poet of the Middle Ages in Europe, just as Homer was the poet of the heroic age of Greece, and Virgil was the Roman poet of the Empire. It has been said that in Dante ten centuries found a voice. Dante was the direct product of mediæval Christianity. In those ten centuries ancient art and learning had been buried in barbarism, and had begun to

trick their beams, and with new spangled ore,
Flame in the forehead of the morning sky.

Christianity had met a new rival in the East, whose sword had desolated the Eastern Empire, whose horse hoofs had violated every sanctuary of the Eastern Church, and who had provoked to new zeal and valour the paladins of Western Europe. The Crusades had brought to Italy and France the spoils of art, luxury, and science; Hildebrand had raised up the Roman Church to be a rival of the Empire of Charlemagne, and Barbarossa had revived an imperial autocracy that eventually should extort at Anagni just retribution for the presumptuous display of arrogance at Canossa. Monasticism had manifested its purest, most practical, and most splendid developments as the cherisher of arts, letters, and the spiritual life. Finally, scholasticism had crystallised the Christian intellectualism of the Western Church, and under its stamp the new-born Roman language acquired the copiousness of the tongue of Cicero, the flexibility and precision of the language of Plato.

On one point in particular Dante was very far removed from both Homer and Virgil. In Greek and Latin literature philosophy was kept quite distinct from all works of the imagination. The atmosphere of the poems of Homer and Virgil is mythology. The supernatural powers that watch the contest on the windy plain of Troy, as well as those which espouse or oppose the voyage of Æneas, are creatures of the imagination, personifications of the powers of nature, of chance, fate, or war. There is no attempt to give an account of the great questions of man's destiny, his nature as a moral being, nor to trace causation in natural phenomena or the progress of human events. Homer's aim is to glorify Greece by describing the valour and grace of a representative Greek, the young, the fateful, the irresistible warrior Achilles. Virgil was a court poet whose object was to celebrate the grandeur of Rome and to flatter the vanity of the house of Augustus.

Dante's object was to give a description of the human race and its destiny. The externalism of the Greek and Latin writers concentrated their attention on the powers of nature as manifested in the beauty and order, as well as in the irresistible forces of the material world. In conflict or harmony with these were represented the activities of the human race. To the Greek, man, in his instincts and appetites, his skill and courage, may appear as the conqueror of nature, whose inextinguishable and essential powers are still personified as gods. The will of these gods was, to the Greek mind, capricious; they eyed human prosperity with jealousy, and punished by a Nemesis the exuberant and overweening satisfaction of human success. But it is extremely important to notice that behind and above both gods and men lay the inscrutable and omnipotent dominion of fate or necessity, the insoluble mystery which both men and gods might look up to and regard with a shudder of helpless apprehension. This inexplicable and awful Judge and

Destroyer, holding in his hands the thread of every law and power in the universe, overshadowed the splendour and glory of the Greek pantheon, and lent an element of instability and change to palaces of Olympus as well as to the reign and dominion of Crœsus or Darius. It seems as if here is the sole point on which religion, as we understand it, entered into the strange poetic creed of Hellenism, and by entering finally succeeded in destroying its charm and its spell of influence, and in drawing the Greek intellect to those profound and long extended philosophical investigations in which final causes were sought after, but never discovered.

Dante wrote at an age when the intellectual world held that it had discovered all, and that all had become so clear and positive a possession of the human mind that the most abstruse questions of God's will and nature, man's moral constitution and eternal destiny, were capable of being treated of in poetry with as much clearness, interest, and vivacity as the battles of Hector, the storm-tossed galleys of Æneas, or the beauty and valour of Camilla.

—Epiphanius Wilson, *Dante Interpreted* (New York: Putnam's, 1899), pp. 44–48

JOHN ADDINGTON SYMONDS ON THE COMPLEXITIES OF
THE DIVINE COMEDY

[John Addington Symonds (1840–1893) was an important literary scholar and lecturer at Oxford University. He wrote *Studies of the Greek Poets* (1873), *Christopher Marlowe* (1887), and other works, but he is best known for his exhaustive study, *The Renaissance in Italy* (1875–86). In this extract from his book on Dante, Symonds comments on the scale and complexity of *The Divine Comedy*.]

Dante did not, like Homer and Milton, set forth the subject of his epic in the first lines of the poem. This has been the source of much confusion and perplexity to critics. For when a poet of the quality of Dante, one of the supreme triad of epic singers, the interpreter of a chaotic middle age, the emerger from barbarian darkness and the babel of confounded dialects, the hierophant of novel mysteries and herald of a world's awakening, the voice that startled Europe from her somnambulism of a thousand years—when such a potent spirit sets himself to condense the whole political, religious, moral, and philosophical experience of his times into a work of art, the sense of which, in his own words, "is by no means simple, nay, rather may be called polysensous, or of many senses," discoverable mainly by four methods of interpretation, "literal, allegorical, moral, anagogical," as is explained in the *Epistle to Can Grande*—can we wonder that the critics are confounded? The cathedral of Dante's building is too vast for comprehension at a glance; and, as is the case with Gothic architecture, unwary observers easily mistake its efflorescences and decorations for the main design, not dreaming that a skeleton of solid structure underlies the whole. Boccaccio, staring at this mighty pile, when its masonry was new and its frescoes still unfaded, pronounced that Dante had erected it solely as a gallows for the better gibbeting of his political antagonists. With this verdict posterity cannot agree. We stand farther off from the aisles and buttresses; we see what Boccaccio does not seem to have noticed, that the spire shoots upwards into bluest sky, taking the hues of evening and of dawn unheeded, when our fields beneath are dim with mists and dew. The ghastly decapitated limbs and grinning heads of Dante's victims do indeed make hideous gargoyles for the water-spouts and writhing corbels for the arches. But we know that these are details subordinate to some more universal plan. Else how should we be reading Dante's poem now? Positive philosophers, who have dispensed with a God or a Gospel, study, it is said, these cantos daily, drawing spiritual sustenance from them. How should they do this, were the juices but the acid sap of envy, malice, and an exile's spite? No; it required the purblindness of a contemporary to accept this view of the *Divine Comedy*. But, says another interpreter, the poem is a huge political pamphlet, an allegorical attack on Guelfism. Exclude all thoughts but this when you approach the three Cantiche, and you will find pitfalls of meaning hidden in each line, subtle disguises, labyrinths conducting to one centre. We have gained a step here. Dante, it is certain, had his Ghibelline antipathies for ever within view. Whatever else may occupy his mind, he never omits to gird at Florence, France, and the Papacy, the three heads of the Guelf faction. He breaks off his description of the celestial rose in order to exalt Henry and abuse Boniface: he points an epigram against his country in the very presence-chamber and before the throne of God. But this interpretation by itself will not suffice. Something broader, of more universal human interest than that old strife of Pope and Emperor, must animate the *Comedy* and be the salt of its immortal life.

—John Addington Symonds, An Introduction to the Study of Dante (New York: Macmillan, 1899), pp. 99–101

KARL VOSSLER ON THE PURPOSE AND STRUCTURE OF *THE DIVINE COMEDY*

[Karl Vossler (1872–1949) was a prolific German critic who wrote *The Spirit of Language in Civilization* (1932) and many other works. In the following extract, Vossler notes that Dante's poem is not designed as a tool for religious conversion but is instead a work of great "spiritual intensity." Vossler then considers the tripartite structure of the poem.]

The construction of the *Commedia,* regarded in and for itself, and judged in accordance with present-day ideals, is essentially dogmatic. But for us the question is whether it is so intended within the *Commedia* itself. Dogmatic arrangement and plan characterized the great theologians, from the apostle Paul down to Thomas Aquinas, for they wished to defend, strengthen, and disseminate their Christian belief. The *Divine Comedy,* however, is evidently intended to convert no heathen, to refute no heretic, to convince no doubter, to contend with no scoffer, to carry on no battle for the faith. Here and there polemic and didactic intentions emerge from it, but they run their course, one and all, within the Christian community, and never is there to be noted an assault or sally against the heathen. There is not even a rallying-cry for a crusade against Islam.

In a future life, where every dispute as to belief is fundamentally, finally, and victoriously settled, dogmatism can serve only for exposition, and can have only representative significance. It does actually figure at once as foundation, support, and decoration for the realms of the Hereafter, as background or scenery, and is therefore within the *Commedia,* in its intention, no theological, ecclesiastical, or philosophical, but an essentially æsthetic, element, and cannot, therefore, be ignored or mentally omitted from the poem as something unpoetic, or only half poetic.

To be sure, there may be an unfortunate stiffness, poetic harshness, or technical arbitrariness, in short, a certain incongruity with the impulses of a life and a pilgrimage conducted through the geometric and astronomic realms of fantasy. Let us look more closely.

The poem actually begins with a sort of arbitrary assumption, namely, with the leap from the Here to the Hereafter, or with the dual character of Dante, who is transformed from the born Florentine that he is into the wandering spirit that he would fain be, and, by means of the poem, becomes. This arbitrary assumption, this dualism, is, however, nothing more than the determination to go forth out of himself, to uplift his spirit, to drop everyday tasks, to seize the golden lyre, and to begin this poem.

> Midway upon the journey of our life
> I found myself within a forest dark,
> For the straightforward pathway had been lost.

It is as if in sleep he had gone astray and missed his true path. "Midway upon the journey of life" means, for Dante, as we learn from the *Convivio,* IV, 24, the age of thirty-five years. And the "dark forest," as can be seen from the same passage, betokens the aberrations of our nature, and deviations from the path of virtue and of truth.

The wanderer then, if we take him literally, moves upon two roads at once: upon the natural path of his years, and upon the moral pathway of life. The contradiction is not removed by the fact that the first path is characterized as a route (*cammino*) and the second as a way (*via*): for the road of life does not primarily stand in any visible relation to the way of personality or character. The first runs toward old age or death as its goal, the second toward sin or virtue.

But the further we read and the more we come under the sway of the poetry, the more what seemed to be merely set down and uttered as something foreign reveals itself as the great ethical act of the will, poetically realized: to escape from the dust of earth and rise aloft above self. So, read in the light of the poem as a whole, these opening verses, which, taken by themselves, are not especially effective, become truly "wingéd words."

We must set value on the mighty and, if you will, harsh opening notes of the Dantesque *Commedia,* for we are dealing with a poem of the highest ethical and spiritual intensity, not with a pleasant little song. By the upward sweep from the Here to the Hereafter the world of the spirit tears itself loose from earth, and if it is to have a new poetic body of its own, the only connecting links or clamps at the disposal of the architect are at first the abstract aids of numbers, of lines, of mathematics. Out of the dualism brought about by renunciation and flight from the world a new unity must emerge.

So he comes to a divine trinity. The number three is the basic note of his *Commedia.* To the left, Hell; to the right, Paradise; between them, Purgatory; and throughout the whole the chain of the triple rhyme, the *terza rima,* and each of the three chief sections (*cantiche*) is divided into thirty-three cantos, so that the poem consists of ninety-nine cantos, nearly equal in length. An introductory canto, or prologue, completes the tale of one hundred. The fundamental three is connected with the number of the Heavenly spheres: ten. His hundred is made up out of three, ten, and one.

Even if we agree, or concede, that the quantitative units, one, three, and ten, may be derived philosophically or theologically, and, so to speak, are determined *a priori,* that would not suffice to demonstrate that the number of cantos in the *Commedia* must necessarily be one hundred. The poem could just as well consist of ten, three hundred, nine hundred, a thousand, three thousand, or more parts. In short, there remains a certain freedom of choice which it would be hard to eliminate.

—Karl Vossler, *Medieval Culture: An Introduction to Dante and His Times* (1907–10), tr. William Cranston Lawton (London: Constable & Co., 1929), Vol. 2, pp. 210–13

GEORGE SANTAYANA ON PAOLO AND FRANCESCA

[George Santayana (1863–1952) was born in Spain but emigrated to the United States and became a leading philosopher and critic. Among his many works are *The Life of Reason* (1905), *Scepticism and Animal Faith* (1923), and the novel *The Last Puritan* (1935). In this extract, Santayana studies the lovers Paolo and Francesca in the *Inferno,* believing that their punishment is a result of a love that has turned into possessiveness.]

If we were to choose the most fearful of the scenes in the *Inferno,* we should have to choose the story of Ugolino, but this is only a pale recital of what Pisa had actually witnessed.

A more subtle and interesting instance, if a less obvious one, may be found in the punishment of Paolo and Francesca di Rimini. What makes these lovers so wretched in the Inferno? They are still together. Can an eternity of floating on the wind, in each other's arms, be a punishment for lovers? That is just what their passion, if left to speak for itself, would have chosen. It is what passion stops at, and would gladly prolong for ever. Divine judgement has only taken it at its word. This fate is precisely what Aucassin, in the well-known tale, wishes for himself and his sweetheart Nicolette,—not a heaven to be won by renunciation, but the possession, even if it be in hell, of what he loves and fancies. And a great romantic poet, Alfred de Musset, actually upbraids Dante for not seeing that such an eternal destiny as he has assigned to Paolo and Francesca would be not the ruin of their love, but the perfect fulfilment of it. This last seems to be very true; but did Dante overlook the truth of it? If so, what instinct guided him to choose just the fate for these lovers that they would have chosen for themselves?

There is a great difference between the apprentices in life, and the masters,—Aucassin and Alfred de Musset were among the apprentices; Dante was one of the masters. He could feel the fresh promptings of life as keenly as any youngster, or any romanticist; but he had lived these things through, he knew the possible and the impossible issue of them; he saw their relation to the rest of human nature, and to the ideal of an ultimate happiness and peace. He had discovered the necessity of saying continually to oneself: Thou shalt renounce. And for this reason he needed no other furniture for hell than the literal ideals and fulfilments of our absolute little passions. The soul that is possessed by any one of these passions nevertheless has other hopes in abeyance. Love itself dreams of more than mere possession; to conceive happiness, it must conceive a life to be shared in a varied world, full of events and activities, which shall be new and ideal bonds between the lovers. But unlawful love cannot pass out into this public fulfilment. It is condemned to be mere possession—possession in the dark, without an environment, without a future. It is love among the ruins. And it is precisely this that is the torment of Paolo and Francesca— love among the ruins of themselves and of all else they might have had to give to one another. Abandon yourself, Dante would say to us,—abandon yourself altogether to a love that is nothing but love, and you are in hell already. Only an inspired poet could be so subtle a moralist. Only a sound moralist could be so tragic a poet.

—George Santayana, "Dante," *Three Philosophical Poets: Lucretius, Dante, and Goethe* (Cambridge, MA: Harvard University Press, 1910), pp. 117–20

BENEDETTO CROCE ON DANTE'S ACCEPTANCE OF CHRISTIAN DOGMA

[Benedetto Croce (1866–1952) was a pioneering Italian literary critic and author of many works, including *Aesthetics* (1902) and *Poetics* (1936). In this extract from his book on Dante, Croce studies the passage in the *Inferno* describing where those who did not receive baptism are confined: Although Dante acknowledges that many of these individuals are worthy, he accepts Christian teaching that they should be damned.]

The entrance to the Inferno, in accordance with the plan of the poem, is by a gate bearing an announcement partly explanatory and partly terrifying. The moralist begins to exercise his judgment and to graduate the sins and vices of mankind. He places the lazy, the timid, the perpetually irresolute, unfit for good or evil, almost outside of this graduation, according to a fantastic law of retribution. Contempt envelops them, and their true punishment is in the verses which score them forever: "These wretches, who never were alive"; "Who lived without infamy and without praise . . ."; "Displeasing to God and to his enemies . . ."; "Who made through cowardice the great refusal . . ."; "Let us not speak of them, but look and pass on. . . ."

A great river next becomes visible and Dante sees people thronging its banks to pass over. A similar scene depicted by his teacher, Virgil, comes back to the memory of the poet, and he gives a new version of it in a manner between the classical and the mediæval. He takes a figure from the pagan mythology and turns him into a demon of the Christian Inferno, the ferocious old slave-driver Charon, with flaming eyes and hairy, hoary cheeks, imperious, inexorable, implacable. Herds of desperate wretches are subject to his nod and suffer from his blows. It is an imitation of an artist by an artist, but an imitation that replunges the model in the reality of the imagination and brings it forth renewed and refreshed.

The moralist and indeed the theologian begins again with the descent, where are found those who did not receive baptism and did not know the true God. They do not suffer external torments, but a pain that is altogether internal, and waste themselves away in perpetual desire without the light of hope. This is a contradiction of human ethical feeling, a mystery of the divine justice, which Dante does not closely scrutinise and against which he exhibits no feeling of revolt. Virgil, who is among the rejected, becomes deathly pale, and Dante's heart beats, for he realises that these were "people of great value." But the situation is not further probed; there is scarcely an indication of the line upon which it might have been developed and we must remain content with the mere statement of fact. The poetry of the passage shows an equal restraint. A similar dry judgment appears in the scene in the noble castle among the great and wise, at the sight of whom the poet is said to rejoice; admiration, reverence, melancholy, are alluded to, but not represented. Dante will later acquire a very different degree of liberty of movement in this other world which he has imagined. At present it appears oppressed by a rule of theological law. Certain images shine out, here and there an expression assumes a lofty tone: "His aspect was neither sad nor glad" . . . "With slow and heavy eyes," "They spake seldom, with soft voices," "At that sight I exulted within myself. . . ." But catalogues of names are everywhere, hardly varied with an epithet. Even when the poet finds himself received by the master of the loftier song (Homer or Virgil) as a sixth along with the five greatest poets of all time, he does not find adequate images and sentiments; he says that they do him "honour" and that among them they spoke of things as to which "it is as well to be silent here as it was well to speak of them there," showing by the words themselves and their turn of expression that he has not much to say, or does not yet know how to say freely what he would. The vein is still running slow or is clogged.

—Benedetto Croce, The Poetry of Dante (1921), tr. Douglas
Ainslie (New York: Henry Holt & Co., 1922), pp. 105–8

PHILIP H. WICKSTEAD ON DANTE'S PURPOSE IN PORTRAYING HELL

[Philip H. Wickstead (1844–1927) is the author of *Dante and Aquinas* (1911), *The Common Sense of*

Political Economy (1933), and *From* Vita Nuova *to* Paradiso (1922), from which the following extract is taken. Here, Wickstead maintains that Dante's purpose in portraying Hell was to depict the consequences of sin.]

Dante's vision of Hell ⟨. . .⟩ is not so much a warning or a threat as to the consequence of sin as a revelation of its inmost nature; and to reveal the true nature of sin is to reveal the true state of fallen and sinful man. As a presentation of an awful fate that will catch the impenitent sinner hereafter Dante's *Inferno* must rank with other descriptions of hell. As a revelation of what the evil choice is in itself, wherever and whenever made, here or hereafter, it stands alone.

And in like manner Dante's *Purgatorio* reveals not the painful condition on compliance with which heaven is offered to the repentant sinner, but a blessed opportunity of cancelling from within his own evil past. The man who sees where his choice has so identified him with things evil, and so alienated him from things good, that his own record would make a discord with heaven in his soul, is now allowed to build up for himself a new record of passionate self-identification with good which shall utterly annul the record of his former self-surrender to evil and shall construct a record through which "the stream of memory can flow unstained."

In other words, Dante's *Inferno* is a revelation of the false-ness of the values by which we live when we sin. And his *Purgatorio* tells how a new life, lived in tune with a new sense of values, may make our whole consciousness, not only our aspirations and desires, harmonious with the experiences of Eden and of Heaven.

But here (to borrow a technical term from Dante's vocabu-lary) we must be careful to "distinguish." On its own denizens hell has no remedial effect whatever, for it brings no revelation to them. It is the place in which "there is no returning to a right state of will," and to say that there is no possibility of repen-tance in Hell is to say that there can be no changed sense of values, and so no revelation of the true meaning of sin to those who are there. So far Dante was in close accord with the received teaching of his time, and, indeed, with the professed creed of the vast majority of Christians in almost every age. Hell, to Dante as to others, was eternal—not, indeed, in the primary sense of being altogether out of relation to time, without beginning or end, and without any conscious successions, but in the secondary sense of "ever-enduring" and "not subject to essential change." Hell therefore is the place of impenitent sin, in which the sinners, though raging against their accomplices, accusing their ill-luck, or cursing God, their parents, and their kin—

> The human race, the seed from which they grew,
> The hour and place they were begotten in   (Musgrave)

yet never essentially change their ideals. However well they see the folly of what they *did,* they no more feel the vileness or vanity of what they *aimed at* than they did on earth. But the very consistency and force with which Dante holds this belief transforms his vision of Hell into a revelation of the nature of the evil choice itself and of the state of mind that it expresses. And it is this that distinguishes, from the moral and spiritual point of view, Dante's descriptions from those, for instance, of Aquinas or of Bunyan. While they in their delineations of Hell exhaust their genius in the attempt to impress upon us the frightful consequences we shall incur by sin, Dante reveals to us the inherent evilness of the evil choice itself, and turns not only our deliberate will, but our affections and our very passions clean away from it.

—Philip H. Wickstead, *From* Vita Nuova *to* Paradiso (London: Longmans, Green & Co., 1922), pp. 34–37

ERICH AUERBACH ON DANTE'S COSMOS

[Erich Auerbach (1892–1957) was an important German critic who wrote many works, including *Mimesis: The Representation of Reality in Western*

Literature (1953), *Literary Language and Its Public in Late Latin Antiquity and in the Middle Ages* (1965), and *Scenes from the Drama of European Literature* (1984). In this extract from his study of Dante, Auerbach argues that Dante's epic is a reactionary tale that attempted to preserve the view of the cosmos that was so rapidly changing during the Renaissance.]

The *Comedy* represented the physical, ethical, and political unity of the Scholastic cosmos at a time when it was beginning to lose its ideological integrity: Dante took the attitude of a conservative defender, his battle was an attempt to regain something that had already been lost; in this battle he was defeated, and his hopes and prophecies were never fulfilled. True, ideas of a Roman World Empire survived down to the Late Renaissance, and indignation over the corruption of the Church led to the great movements of the Reformation and Counter Reformation. But those ideas and movements have only certain superficial characteristics in common with Dante's view of the world; they originated and grew independently of it. Some were fantastic dreams, some were great popular uprisings, some acts of practical politics, and still others had something of all three: but none possessed the depth and universal unity of Dante's Thomist world view, and their consequence was not the worldwide *humana civilitas* for which Dante hoped, but an increasing fragmentation of cultural forces; it is only after the imperial ideology and the Christian-medieval conception of the world, shaken by intestine struggles, were swept away by the rationalism of the seventeenth and eighteenth centuries that a new practical view of the unity of human society began to take form. Thus Dante's work remained almost without influence on the history of European thought; immediately after his death, and even during his lifetime, the structure of literary, cultured society underwent a complete change in which he had no part, the change from Scholastic to Humanistic thinking, and that transformation undermined the influence of so rigorously committed a work as the *Comedy*. The radical shift in values that has taken place is made clear by the example of Petrarch, who was only forty years younger than Dante. Petrarch was not actually of a different party, he was not opposed to Dante's strivings; but what moved Dante, the whole attitude and form of his life, had grown alien to him. He is distinguished from Dante above all by his new attitude toward his own person; it was no longer in looking upward—as Orcagna portrayed Dante in his fresco of the Last Judgment in Santa Maria Novella—that Petrarch expected to find self-fulfillment, but in the conscious cultivation of his own nature. Although far inferior to Dante in personality and natural endowment, he was unwilling to acknowledge any superior order or authority; not even the authority of the universal world order to which Dante submitted so passionately. The autonomous personality, of which Petrarch was to be the first fully typical modern European embodiment, has lived in a thousand forms and varieties; the conception takes in all the tendencies of the modern age, the business spirit, the religious subjectivism, the humanism, and the striving for physical and technological domination of the world. It is incomparably richer, deeper, and more dangerous than the ancient cult of the person. From Christianity, whence it rose and which it ultimately defeated, this conception inherited unrest and immoderation. These qualities led it to discard the structure and limits of Dante's world, to which, however, it owed the power of its actuality.

Accordingly, even if it is agreed that Dante's creation is closely bound up with his subject matter, that his poetry is inseparable from his doctrine, he seems to be a special case that has never been repeated and hence tells us nothing about the nature of the poetic process. For the art of imitating reality continued to develop quite independently of the presuppositions which seem to have been at the base of Dante's work. No poet or artist after Dante required an ultimate, eschatological destiny in order to perceive the unity of the human person: sheer intuitive power seems to have enabled subsequent writers to combine inner and outward observation into a whole.

—Erich Auerbach, *Dante: Poet of the Secular World* (1929), tr. Ralph Manheim (Chicago: University of Chicago Press, 1961), pp. 175–77

❖

[T. S. Eliot (1888–1965), an American-born writer who spent most of his adult life in England, was not only one of the leading modernist poets of his age but also a leading critic. His works of criticism include *The Sacred Wood* (1920) and *On Poetry and Poets* (1957). In this extract from his monograph on Dante, Eliot explores Dante's philosophical and theological beliefs.]

The allegory in the *Inferno* was easy to swallow or ignore, because we could, so to speak, grasp the concrete end of it, its solidification into imagery; but as we ascend from Hell to Heaven we are more and more required to grasp the whole from idea to image.

Here I must make a diversion, before tackling a specifically philosophical passage of the *Purgatorio,* concerning the nature of Belief. I wish merely to indicate certain tentative conclusions of my own, which might affect one's reading of the *Purgatorio.*

Dante's debt to St. Thomas Aquinas, like his debt (a much smaller one) to Virgil, can be easily exaggerated; for it must not be forgotten that Dante read and made use of other great mediaeval philosophers as well. Nevertheless, the question of how much Dante took from Aquinas and how much from elsewhere is one which has been settled by others and is not relevant to my present essay. But the question of what Dante 'believed' is always relevant. It would not matter, if the world were divided between those persons who are capable of taking poetry simply for what it is and those who cannot take it at all; if so, there would be no need to talk about this question to the former and no use in talking about it to the latter. But most of us are somewhat impure and apt to confuse issues: hence the justification of writing books about books, in the hope of straightening things out.

My point is that you cannot afford to *ignore* Dante's philosophical and theological beliefs, or to skip the passages which express them most clearly; but that on the other hand you are not called upon to believe them yourself. It is wrong to think that there are parts of the *Divine Comedy* which are of interest only to Catholics or to mediaevalists. For there is a difference (which here I hardly do more than assert) between philosophical *belief* and poetic *assent*. I am not sure that there is not as great a difference between philosophical belief and scientific belief; but that is a difference only now beginning to appear, and certainly inapposite to the thirteenth century. In reading Dante you must enter the world of thirteenth-century Catholicism, which is not the world of modern Catholicism, as his world of physics is not the world of modern physics. You are not called upon to believe what Dante believed, for your belief will not give you a groat's worth more of understanding and appreciation; but you are called upon more and more to understand it. If you can read poetry as poetry, you will 'believe' in Dante's theology exactly as you believe in the physical reality of his journey; that is, you suspend both belief and disbelief. I will not deny that it may be in practice easier for a Catholic to grasp the meaning, in many places, than for the ordinary agnostic; but that is not because the Catholic believes, but because he has been instructed. It is a matter of knowledge and ignorance, not of belief or scepticism. The vital matter is that Dante's poem is a whole; that you must in the end come to understand every part in order to understand any part.

Furthermore, we can make a distinction between what Dante believes as a poet and what he believed as a man. Practically, it is hardly likely that even so great a poet as Dante could have composed the *Comedy* merely with understanding and without belief; but his private belief becomes a different thing in becoming poetry. It is interesting to hazard the suggestion that this is truer of Dante than of any other philosophical poet. With Goethe, for instance, I often feel too acutely 'this is what Goethe the man believed', instead of merely entering into a world which Goethe has created; with Lucretius also; less with the *Bhagavad-Gita,* which is the next greatest philosophical poem to the *Divine Comedy* within my experience. That is the advantage of a coherent traditional system of dogma and morals like the Catholic: it stands apart, for understanding and assent even without belief, from the single individual who propounds it. Goethe always arouses in me a strong sentiment of disbelief in what he believes: Dante does not. I believe that this is because Dante is the purer poet, not because I have more sympathy with Dante the man than Goethe the man.

—T. S. Eliot, *Dante* (London: Faber & Faber, 1929), pp. 34–37

Dorothy L. Sayers on Comedy in *The Divine Comedy*

[Dorothy L. Sayers (1893–1957), one of the most famous writers of detective fiction in the "Golden Age" of the 1920s and 1930s, became a theologian and Dante scholar in later life. Aside from translating *The Divine Comedy,* she wrote two volumes of papers on Dante. In this extract, Sayers champions the humorous aspects of *The Divine Comedy,* which she feels have been largely ignored by critics.]

There is, it is true, another kind of laughter in Dante—a laughter which shocks and scarifies; the laughter which people like John Jay Chapman have in mind when they say that Dante's "attempts at humour are lamentable". But this kind is not humour at all, nor meant to be—it is the terrible satiric laughter, the laughter of a Dean Swift, bitter and coarse and cruel. Dante can wield that great lash—but, true enough, it does not make us smile. It is intended to make us wince, and it does. Only a very few poets, and those the greatest, have both kinds of laughter at command. The same hand that wrote *Timon of Athens* wrote *The Tempest,* but Swift cannot write like Jane Austen, nor Jane Austen like Swift. Dante, who outgoes the one in strength and the other in tenderness, is one of the great ones; and it is only when one has understood his mocking gentleness that one can admire, or even abide, his ruthless mockery.

The whip—as is fitting—cracks loudest in Hell; that is why it is often supposed to be more characteristic of Dante than the other laughter, since twenty people have skimmed through the *Inferno* for one who has read the *Purgatorio* or the *Paradiso.* It makes an ugly noise—but Hell is full of ugly noises: that is its nature. We are all still unconsciously influenced by Byron, and disposed to believe that the Prince of Darkness is a gentleman. Dante knew better. He knew that for all his façade of dark beauty, proud defiance, and stoicism in suffering, the Devil is a fool, and a vulgar fool at that. With a kind of ghastly buffoonery, he strips away the exterior show and displays the disgusting and ridiculous fact of evil. The demons of the Fifth Bolgia are grotesque and detestable—rat-catchers in a sewer; and the rats themselves are no better. All are tarred with the same pitch. ⟨. . .⟩ The devils fork up Ciampolo—streaming, shining, sleeked head to heel in the black pitch, "looking like an otter". He whines and jeers; they pull bits off him, like nasty children tormenting flies; he offers to betray his fellow-sinners; the devils fall for the trick; he escapes and they turn tooth and nail on one another; they tumble into the pitch and are left squabbling and scalding. "*O tu che leggi, udirai nuovo ludo*". But there is nothing here for smiles, or for the thing called a "sense of humour". What laughter there is, when Hell thus preys on Hell, is of a dreadful sort: "He that dwelleth in the Heavens shall laugh them to scorn; the Lord shall have them in derision."

Hell preys on Hell—Hell gibes at Hell: in the "bottom of sin" there is neither humanity nor sympathy nor decency. The traitors hasten to denounce one another, and their brutal witticisms echo under the stone vault and over the unyielding ice. ⟨. . .⟩ If we want to know whether we are expected to find these sour japes humorous, or even agreeable, we may turn back to the end of the 30th Canto, where Dante stands, all agog, listening to Sinon and Master Adam, "between whom" (in the words of Dante's nineteenth-century translator, the Rev. Ichabod Wright, a respectable Oxford don, who should have known better), "takes place a most comical dialogue." Neither Dante's absorption, nor (one may imagine) Mr. Wright's idea of fun, wins any approval from Virgil: "*chè voler ciò udire è basso voglio*—It's vulgar to enjoy that kind of thing."

What hampers the Anglo-Saxon in his judgment of satiric poetry is his fixed idea that all laughter ought to be kindly and all humour good-humoured. If he combines with this the notion that all religion ought to be sweetly consolatory and perfectly refined and "nice", and the humanistic delusion that wickedness is more a misfortune than a fault, he will find himself in a position where he is hopelessly out of key—not only with Dante, but also with both the Old Testament and the New. If his critical judgment is not to be seriously impaired, he must, while reading the *Commedia,* accept the central Christian affirmations—that holiness is a joy to those that love it and a horror to those that hate it; that sin is a hideous illusion and Hell the wilful persistence in that illusion; that Redemption is bought with blood and tears; that Love is most truly a "lord of terrible aspect". He must not take evil lightly, but know it as the proper object—indeed the only proper object—of the emotions of wrath and scorn.

Between this satiric laughter and the laughter that arises from the sense of the comic there is a great gulf fixed. Both, indeed, arise from an apprehension of Man's inadequacy: his pretensions are so vast and his nature so limited; his immortal destiny so high and his mortal achievements so petty. But there the likeness ends. The comic spirit can afford to be indulgent to man, because, when all is said and done, it rates him but as a poor creature from whom little is to be expected. It looks on him and all his works as Dr. Johnson looked on learned women or dogs walking on their hind legs—the thing is not well done but it is a marvel that it is done at all. Indeed, without God's grace, it never can be done. But satire looks upon man in his noblest potentiality, and rages that he should fall so short of his divine self. It is aware of the profound tragedy of the human situation, and its harsh laughter bears witness to an agony of the spirit. One might say of satire that it is the exact inverse of the spirit of high comedy: that it is a form of tragedy, "*qui côtoie sans cesse le tragique et n'y tombe jamais*" ⟨"which constantly skirts tragedy but never falls into it"⟩.

—Dorothy L. Sayers, "The Comedy of the Comedy," *Introductory Papers on Dante* (London: Methuen, 1954), pp. 166–69

[Charles S. Singleton (1909–1985), formerly a professor of English at Johns Hopkins University, was a leading Dante scholar. Aside from writing an extensive commentary (with English translation) of *The Divine Comedy*, he wrote *Journey to Beatrice* (1957) and *An Essay on the* Vita Nuova (1958) and edited *Art, Science, and History of the Renaissance* (1967). In this extract, Singleton examines Dante's poetic vision of religious mythology.]

Would it not have been simpler, one may ask, to have said right off that we were talking of religious myth? Perhaps. Only just what that would have explained about Brunetto Latini in Hell is not clear. It is commonly said that Dante put his enemies in Hell. And indeed he did. But to put it that way is only another way out of facing the myth directly. Again that puts the problem on Dante and puts it in terms which our shifting relativistic modern mind is all too ready to take refuge in. For it needs be said that Dante put his friends in Hell too. There is no reason at all to believe that Dante did not love Brunetto as he might have loved a father. There is every reason to believe that, had it depended on him, Dante would have had Brunetto in Paradise. But what I am trying to account for (and what the term religious myth might not account for in this case) is this: *that it does not depend on Dante.* This is a vision, not of things as we should wish them to be, but of things as they are. These are things which, even before they are seen, are submitted to the lap of God; and because of this, when they are seen, they are objective. They do not stand in illusory space. They stand in a space that God sees. To remember St. Paul, they are known even as we are known. Does the author of Genesis want God to create beasts and man on the sixth day rather than another? Or does God walk in the garden in the cool of the evening because the author likes the idea? Again we answer question with question. But sometimes that is the best way—or perhaps the only way.

As for Dante, I am here talking about a quality of vision which becomes a pervading quality of his poetry. To anyone who knows his poem well it amounts to a steady feeling that somehow beyond his words there is a reality which would remain even if the words were taken away. And I am looking for a formula which will account psychologically for this quality in Dante. I think we had one back along our path when we talked of Aquinas and the position of philosophy in the Middle Ages. It was a well-worn formula which one recognized immediately: *fides quaerens intellectum,* faith seeking understanding. Or there is another version: *praecedit fides, sequitur intellectus,* faith goes ahead, understanding follows. Now if I may be allowed to alter these formulae ever so little, we shall have one to account for the quality I speak of in Dante's poem. I would suggest: *fides quaerens visionem; praecedit fides, sequitur visio.* And this, I submit, fits not only a quality in Dante but the myth of Genesis and Plato's myth. There may be others that one would want to add to the list. But I suspect they are not many. There are no others in Italian literature either before or after Dante. Neither in Petrarch nor in Tasso nor in Leopardi does faith move before the tongue moves or the eye sees. Petrarch's space of imagination is already a space of illusion. He and the others belong to the Renaissance and aesthetics can perhaps claim to deal with them. But aesthetics as the science of the beautiful can never deal with Plato's myth or Genesis or Dante's poem. For they aim neither at beauty (not first of all) nor illusion. Theirs is a vision of an objective order of things in its goodness and its rightness. And for them anything short of this were ugliness.

—Charles S. Singleton, *Dante Studies, Volume 1:* Commedia, *Elements of Structure* (Cambridge, MA: Harvard University Press, 1954), pp. 80–82

IRMA BRANDEIS ON BEATRICE

[Irma Brandeis (1906–1990) was a translator, lecturer, and Dante scholar at Bard College. In this extract from

So much has been written about this lady, she has been so laden with theories, printed notes, summaries and arguments, that it has become almost impossible for the present-day student of Dante to see her freshly as the text of the poem presents her. This situation is complicated by the undeniable fact that the totally uninstructed approach has great drawbacks, too. We cannot comprehend the Beatrice Dante had in mind without some notion of the mediaeval conceptions of woman and of love; we ought to know something of the poetry that preceded Dante's; and we need to have our eyes filled with mediaeval pictorial art, so that we will not visualize the scene in the Terrestrial Paradise in terms that give a false qualification (however beautiful) to the substance of Dante's vision.

Still, the reader who has little experience of these things can, if he hangs on closely to Dante's text, see the real outlines of the Beatrice image, and feel its poetry. He has chiefly to listen attentively to everything Dante says, and as carefully to avoid interpretations that contradict the spirit of the text or the important details of its letter. Dante is not careless or inconsequential: he says nothing unintentionally; and, since he wants us to know his meaning, he posts his poem with clues that can lead us to it. If that is so, whatever symbolic significance Beatrice is meant to have will be implicit in her whole figure and action, from the girlhood of the *Vita Nuova* onward, and will be capable of being *felt* as well as understood, without discords or contradictions. If we assume that this is so, we will not be tempted by artificial and academic interpretations or simple, sentimental ones, and will not seek a "meaning" for Beatrice which is not promoted by the text out of which she emerges. Above all, we will avoid the deadly mistake of equating her with some noble and chill abstract concept, as at times it has been the fashion to do. For there is nothing to be gained but falsification and diminishment of Dante's poetry by interpreting Beatrice as an allegorical representation of Theology or Divine Revelation, or any other abstraction of the sort. To do so requires that one ignore a great many things that Dante is at pains to impress on us (for surely it was not Theology with which Dante fell in love at the age of nine, nor Revelation which descended into Hell to send Virgil to the rescue, saying "It was love that moved me and that makes me speak")—and above all, the exalted praise for the capacities of the human soul which is implied in her whole role. As Etienne Gilson says,

> If Beatrice is only a symbol, she is a symbol whose body, after its death, was brought to earth, where it resides at the time when Dante was writing these lines (*Purg.* XXXI, 49–51) in expectation of its future glorification. We are assuredly yielding to the most urgent suggestions of Dante himself if we see in Beatrice a human being composed like us of a soul and a body, her soul being in heaven and her body on earth; a being who, since she is actually dead, has actually lived.

This does not mean that the figure of Beatrice has no symbolic import, but merely that it cannot have one which contradicts the living past described in the *Vita Nuova* and recalled vividly in the Terrestrial Paradise. The risen and glorified Beatrice whom the protagonist had loved during the brief lifetime described in the early book, and who is the agent of his rescue in the *Comedy,* is a figure that brims with significance. Her role is that of a mediator between human and divine things. She is, as Virgil calls her, "a light between truth and intellect". But nothing in Dante's text or in his philosophy of composition will justify us in so forgetting the details of her well-established identity as to equate her with an abstraction, whatever its magnificence.

—Irma Brandeis, *The Ladder of Vision: A Study of Dante's* Comedy (Garden City, NY: Anchor Books, 1962), pp. 114–16

THOMAS GODDARD BERGIN ON THE DEMOGRAPHY OF HELL

[Thomas Goddard Bergin (1904–1987), formerly Sterling Professor of Romance Languages at Yale University, wrote *Dante* (1965), *Perspectives on the Divine Comedy* (1967), and *A History of Italian Literature* (1974). In this extract, Bergin studies the individuals who are found in Dante's Hell, noting that they are a mixture of classical and Italian individuals, most of whom are men.]

By my count, there are 164 definitely named or easily identified characters in the *Inferno*. (I count here only residents and not figures merely alluded to.) Of these, some eighty are from the classical world, four may be thought of as biblical, and the rest are largely from Dante's own contemporary society, though we must allow ourselves a little freedom in the definition of this area. The mingling of these various sects is not without its purpose. Putting together such figures as Judas on the one hand and Brutus and Cassius on the other is in line with our poet's deliberate and self-conscious historical syncretism, the principal cultural intention of the *Comedy*, which is sharpened here if we recall that Satan is the third element of the group: Old Testament, New Testament, and classical betrayers meet at the center of the universe. But I think that in the *Inferno* Dante is not so much concerned with the blending of the classical and the Judeo-Christian traditions as such (this is more marked in the *Purgatorio*, though since he cannot bring it out in the characters of the narrative it has to be emphasized in the embellishment and the collateral rhetoric) as with blending antiquity and the present into one homogeneous family of man. It has been frequently observed, in this connection, that Dante creates his own "exemplary figures"; characters such as Francesca and Ugolino have all the eternal mythopoeic virtue of any character from Homer or Sophocles. It is less commonly noted that his strategy has both fronts in mind: Ulysses, Jason, and Alexander mingle, not unobtrusively perhaps, but in a quite familiar fashion, with sly plotters from Romagna, Bolognese seducers, or petty Italian tyrants. Dante's own familiarity with Virgil has a unique immediacy and spontaneity. The poet uses his own person as a symbol of the present confronting the past, with reverence always but with no abdication of personality. So Myrrha and Gianni Schicchi are seen as two of a kind, Pier da Medicina introduces Curio with a kind of ferocious camaraderie, and Sinon and Maestro Adamo belabor each other with intimate invective, caricaturing at the same time that they stress the syncretistic intent of the poem. No wonder Dante listens with rapt attention! Only in the *Inferno* is such magnificent cosmopolitanism possible.

Among the nonclassical figures resident in Hell the preponderance is Italian. I count sixty-four Italians as against sixteen others in this general category (excluding the four biblical figures). Perhaps here it should be noted that in the large, anonymous, vaguely estimated groups, Italians also have a disproportionate representation; it would seem that numerous *Lucchesi* and Sardinians swim in the pitch of the barrators, and Caccianemico clearly implies that the Bolognese are well represented among the panders. Florence's name is, as we remember, "spread through Hell," by now comfortably stocked with Pisans and Genoese too, if we are to put faith in the poet's invectives. In any event, of the sixty-four Italians specifically named the majority (forty-one) are Tuscan, and of these, twenty-six are Florentines. (Our figures include the otherwise unidentified "ancient of St. Zita" of Canto XXI, and the anonymous but clearly Florentine suicide of Canto XIII.) Tuscans also have the widest spread of all Hell's delegations: we find two of them among the incontinent, three among the heretics, thirteen with the violent, no less than fourteen included in the impartially fraudulent (representing five of the ten Malebolge), and a respectable quota of nine authentic traitors. Not even the classical delegates, all taken together, have such a wide range, though they come close: of them I find five incontinent, one heretic (we know Epicurus is there although we do not actually see his tomb), six violent, twelve in the Malebolge (though representing six pouches), and two arch-traitors (or three, if we assume, as perhaps we should, that Antenor has come to rest in the ice-zone that bears his name). When it comes to speaking parts, the Tuscans have twenty-one out of the entire sixty-five (or sixty-six if Paolo speaks the vindictive line "Caina awaits"; some have thought so and it is an attractive notion). Of course, as Dante recurrently makes clear, it is natural that Tuscans should speak more readily than the rest; after all, their visitor and interlocutor is a compatriot. On the subject of Tuscans, and in a larger way Italians, it is interesting to note how many are related: there are three of the Cavalcanti tribe; two, possibly three, Pazzi; two of either the Abati or Donati, depending on the identity of Buoso of Canto XXV; two Ubaldini; and no less than four of the illustrious clan of the Conti Guidi. Some of them have kinsmen in the other realms too, the house of Swabia and (by now) the Donati are represented in all three kingdoms. But our pilgrim will meet only six more fellow-townsmen over the rest of his journey; Hell, the most generous of the realms in its admission policy, is also, in respect to Dante's contacts, the most homelike. ⟨. . .⟩

The sex census is not without interest. Hell is pretty solidly a man's world; of all the characters even so much as mentioned, only twenty-four are women and, of these, fifteen are Limbo dwellers and so merely names. Of the remaining nine, it is interesting to note that all but one (Manto) have some erotic significance: they include one prostitute and seven illicit lovers. The nature of the sins of Myrrha and Potiphar's wife puts them among the falsifiers for purposes of Dante's categories, but their motivation is lust. There are no women in all the circles of the violent, none in Cocytus; they seem also to have been innocent of gluttony, avarice, and seven out of ten of the lesser kinds of fraud. Even in general categories Dante speaks of them only twice; there are *femmine* in the Limbo and sorry witches among the soothsayers. (Indeed Dante is probably showing his medievalism in this area.) In the *Inferno,* we may add, the only female resident with a speaking part is Francesca (for Beatrice is a transient and Thaïs is merely quoted). There are no children at all (there is nothing, happily, to make us think that Ugolino's sons are Hell dwellers) save for the anonymous *infanti* of Limbo, more tenderly referred to by Virgil as "innocent little ones" in the *Purgatorio,* balancing, as Dante's love for symmetry would require, the "childish voices" of the lower tiers of the celestial rose.

—Thomas Goddard Bergin, "Hell: Topography and Demography" (1965), *A Diversity of Dante* (New Brunswick, NJ: Rutgers University Press, 1969), pp. 56–60

ROBERT HOLLANDER ON THE ULYSSES-MOTIF IN *THE DIVINE COMEDY*

[Robert Hollander (b. 1933) is the author of *Studies in Dante* (1980), *Dante and Paul's "Five Words with*

Understanding" (1992), and *Dante's Epistle to Cangrande* (1993). In the following extract from *Allegory in Dante's* Commedia (1969), Hollander examines the twenty-sixth canto of the *Inferno,* which concerns Ulysses, and finds the Ulysses-motif to be a dominant one in the entire work.]

The canto of Ulysses has much in common with that of Francesca; it even happens to contain the same number of lines (142). And like that earlier canto, it begins relatively slowly and quietly (as does the Farinata canto), preparing us for the enormous experience we are about to witness. As in the Francesca canto over one-half of the canto is preparation; indeed, the epic, uninterrupted speech of Ulysses only begins at line 90, and is thus limited to a mere fifty-three lines.

The Ulysses-motif is one of the strongest and most deeply felt in the *Commedia.* In *Inferno* it establishes the voyage theme which will be the dominant motif for the poem itself as it rises toward its conclusion. The Ulysses-motif also, I believe, points us back not only to the inception of the poem, but to the experiences that Dante invokes at the commencement of his work and that refer to the types of his own experience as these have been recorded in previous literature. For this study I am primarily interested in the conclusion of Ulysses' speech; and in order to reach it, I should like to notice three passages on the way.

The Ulysses canto begins by concluding the previous canto with the bitterly ironic address to Florence, whose fame is spread abroad in Hell. As Dante and Virgil descend, the Poet interrupts the action to make the following comment:

> Allor mi dolsi, e ora mi ridoglio
>   quando drizzo la mente a ciò ch'io vidi,
>   e più lo 'ngegno affreno ch'i' non soglio,
> perché non corra che virtù nol guidi;
>   sì che, se stella bona o miglior cosa
>   m'ha dato 'l ben, ch'io stessi nol m'invidi.
>
> [I felt grief then, and feel grief now again
>   when I turn my mind to what I saw,
>   and more than I am wont I rein my talent in

lest it run where virtue guide it not,
    so that, if kindly star or better thing
    has granted me its boon, I need not hold it against myself.]
                                                    (*Inf.* XXVI, 19–24)

It is clear that Dante thinks of Ulysses as one who allowed his considerable powers to run where virtue guided not. He himself, as a man and as a poet, will be charged with the same kind of venturesomeness by Beatrice, probably with specific reference to *Convivio,* although this point is much debated. At any rate, it is a sort of "There but for the Grace of God go I" passage, and serves to introduce the similarity between Dante's past and Ulysses' great adventure which the later passages will clarify by developing.

Next, the Poet keeps us distant from the great Ulysses by making him and his fellows resemble the fireflies of early evening, seen from above by a resting peasant.

—Robert Hollander, *Allegory in Dante's* Commedia (Princeton: Princeton University Press, 1969), pp. 114–16

WILLIAM ANDERSON ON THE MULTIPLICITY OF MEANING IN *THE DIVINE COMEDY*

[William Anderson is the author of *Dante the Maker* (1980), from which the following extract is taken. Here, Anderson explores some of the implications of the last lines of *The Divine Comedy,* finding many levels of interpretation in them.]

In the last lines of the *Commedia,* Dante records the passing of his consciousness into the conscious Love permeating the universe. These lines express the approaching consummation of the greatest theme of his life, the ardent will to love, so evident from his earliest memories of childhood and recurring as his understanding and knowledge of where his love should be directed grew throughout his experience of life. Boccaccio regretted that he had to record Dante's inclination throughout his life to the sin of *lussuria*, or lechery; yet what this probably means is simply that Dante had a strong sexual drive. Indeed it was the tension between his sexuality and his aspiration towards a perfect, rational, and intellectual love that helps to explain the variety, intensity, and amplitude of his creative powers. There is a constant parallel interaction between his sexuality, his artistic creativeness, and his mystical nature. Often these sides of his character were in conflict, and every now and then they formed a unity of experience, each transvalued and changed in the light of consciousness into major works of art.

His falling in love when he was almost nine with the child Beatrice was a mystical experience of enhanced consciousness that transformed, refined and purified the later and more self-acknowledged sexual attraction and the overwhelming emotions to which he gave vent in his verse. When he fell in love, his general awareness changed, altering his perceptions of the external world, deepening his memory and so making all the impressions of life reveal their inner connexions with the aim of his art. Even though I have no more than sketched the capacity of his mind for absorbing knowledge, ideas, and visual, auditory, and tactile information, I hope to have given some outline of what an efficient and retentive mind it was. True art depends on intensity of experience for the impression and effect it makes: intensity of experience depends in turn on the degree of consciousness in the artist at the moment of experience. The grading of the levels of inspirations shown to relate to the journey of the *Commedia* is equally a grading of the transformations of consciousness from the ordinary waking state to a subjective state of fuller awareness and on to an objective state of higher consciousness. Such a change in the state of consciousness, as shown by the examples Dante gives in the *Purgatorio,* releases the imaginative and dream-making mechanisms of the mind, enabling them to form fuller syntheses and more original creations out of the memory and to draw on the deepest resources of symbols in the psyche. The hidden, forgotten sides of the mind respond with gratitude to the light cast upon them and, though some of their gifts may at first seem strange repayments, monsters wrought in darkness, nightmares of cruelty, succubi riding fearful winds, these have other meanings, made clear by the calm interpretative mind relating them to the pattern of the whole. Gradually this awakening of consciousness expands the understanding of particular events and experiences and reveals their universal significance and the part they play in a hitherto veiled pattern. Then enhanced consciousness unlocks the emotional understanding, showing the link between the love of the individual with the love of the universal and enabling the utterance of the poetry of praise.

Dante's relation of his art to the degrees of consciousness gives one reason for the abiding newness and the inexhaustible richness of the *Commedia* because, although his cosmology, many features of his faith, and the preconceptions of his society have now been totally discarded, the problems and mysteries of human consciousness abide with us still. He contained in himself the whole of a culture that has since become divided into the culture of the scientist and the culture of the artist. By taking over the interpretative techniques devised or handed down through monastics, he saved for literature the multiplicity of meanings that was under serious attack from the scholastics. Again, he took the Aristotelian terminology of the scholastics and used it in the cause of his own Neoplatonic tradition to enrich the vocabulary of poetry. He was intensely alive to the great technological innovations of the thirteenth century, to the yoking of new resources of power and machinery, as the references to dykes, windmills, shipping, and horology show, making the *Commedia* a mirror of the bustle and life and the communications of money and trade of Western Europe, creating in the poem a three-dimensional vision of the globe itself waiting to be explored, and uttering the incipient desire to burst the bonds of experience in exploration.

—William Anderson, *Dante the Maker* (London: Routledge & Kegan Paul, 1980), pp. 401–2

[Patrick Boyde, professor elect of Italian at the University of Cambridge and fellow of St. John's College, is a distinguished Dante scholar and author of *Dante's Style in His Lyric Poetry* (1971) and *Perception and Passion in Dante's Comedy* (1993). In this extract from *Dante Philomythes and Philosopher* (1981), Boyde studies the demons in the *Inferno*.]

There remains one last purely Christian or purely religious component in Dante's beliefs concerning the angels. Within a matter of seconds of their creation, he tells us, a large body of the angels, perhaps a tenth of the total number, rose in proud rebellion and were driven out of heaven into the 'pit'. That 'pit' is of course the underworld of Hell; the fallen angels are the devils or demons; and the Devil par excellence is their leader, Lucifer, once the Prince of Light, now the 'Emperor of the Dolorous Realm', where he is known by the new and sinister names of Satan and Beelzebub.

Angels fell from all nine orders. There are nine circles in Dante's Hell. His Satan has the six wings of a Seraph, and a demon from the eighth circle is described as 'one of the black Cherubim'. It is therefore plausible that Dante intended us to deduce that the devils stationed in any one circle are all drawn from one order, and that the sequence of the hierarchies is maintained in such a way that the highest circle is manned by 'legionaries' from the lowest order of angels.

To these nine legions we must add the 'evil choir of angels who were neither rebels to God nor loyal to him, but who stood for themselves':

> . . . quel cattivo coro
> de li angeli che non furon ribelli
> né fur fedeli a Dio, ma per sé fuoro.   (*Inf.* III, 37–9)

Fittingly, 'they too are driven from Heaven in order not to mar its beauty; but they are not received into the depths of Hell, lest the damned should gain some glory from their presence there':

Caccianli i ciel per non esser men belli,
né lo profondo inferno li riceve,
ch'alcuna gloria i rei avrebber d'elli.   (40–2)

Instead they inhabit a no-man's-land, the so-called Vestibule or
Antinferno, which lies between the gate of Hell and the first
coil of the infernal river where Charon ferries the souls over the
Acheron.

There will be no need for us to go deeply into Dante's
demonology. Devils make only one brief appearance in the
action of the *Inferno* until the protagonist reaches the ten
'pockets of evil', or *Malebolge,* which form the penultimate circle; and Dante's inspiration is drawn not from his reading in
theology, but from painting, folk-tales and the popular religious
drama.

The devils are horned, winged, fleet of foot, and sharp of
shoulder. In certain cases they are allowed to go and collect the
souls of the damned from the upper world; and they may even
snatch the soul of a traitor in the very instant of his treachery,
leaving a devil behind to inhabit the body until the day
appointed for its natural death. They will struggle with angels—
another folk-motif—for the possession of a soul whose fate is
uncertain; and while they lose the contest for the young
Buonconte da Montefeltro, a Ghibelline general who died of
wounds received in battle, but who had time to shed a tear of
true repentance before he expired, they triumphantly carry off
the soul of his father, the crafty and calculating Guido, notwithstanding his Franciscan habit and the absolution he had
received from the Pope himself.

In Hell, their task is to oversee the torments of the damned.
They are shown as armed with whips in one instance and with
iron hooks in another. Where the punishment consists of
immersion, they are described as thrusting the souls back
below the surface like cooks prodding meat down into a stew.
Their activities are reported with great gusto in Dante's long
account of his adventures in the fifth *bolgia* where a group of
ten devils, with grotesque names, are allowed to run riot. They
lie to Virgil about the path he should follow; they threaten the
terrified pilgrim; they express themselves in the highly-spiced,

scurrilous language of the Florentine 'underworld'; they catch a sinner, but allow him to slip away; they fight among themselves, until two of them fall into the boiling pitch. They give chase to the two poets, who are forced to make an undignified getaway by sliding down the slope into the next ditch. But the devils' impotence is stressed in our final glimpse of the band as they glare down at their intended victims. They are powerless to pursue their prey any further. Against their will they remain 'ministers of high providence'; and their sphere of action is strictly limited. They are like the gargoyles on a Gothic cathedral, harmless to those who have a clear conscience, and useful in spite of themselves.

In fact, it may not be too far-fetched to claim that all the devils described in the first cantica are there to further the cause of the good. They are as black in appearance and in heart as their heavenly counterparts are white; and they exist in order to sharpen our awareness of the angelic *candore*. Their cruelty should excite a contempt that will enhance our admiration for the gentleness and consideration shown by the guardian angels in Purgatory. And such a deliberate contrast of negative and positive images is nowhere more apparent than in Dante's presentation of Lucifer.

Once the highest of the high, he is now the lowest of the low, a 'vile worm' stuck fast in the very centre of the earth and of the universe, at the furthest point from God. Once the most beautiful being in the whole of creation, he is now revoltingly ugly. He has three heads in a grim parody of the Three-Person God; but the possession of six eyes merely gives him extra vents for his tears, and the three mouths are no longer vehicles of praise, but instruments of torture for the souls of the arch-traitors who are crushed and mauled between his jaws. His three heads are of different colours; but the white, green and red of the theological virtues, or the white, gold and living flame of the angels in heaven, have given place to black, off-yellow and a sinister vermilion. He still retains his six Seraph's wings, but they are bat-like now; and their beating produces neither a gentle breeze with ambrosial fragrance, nor the vivifying breath associated with the Holy Spirit, but a cold wind that turns the last section of the infernal river into the frozen ice of Lake Cocytus.

—Patrick Boyde, *Dante Philomythes and Philosopher: Man in the Cosmos* (Cambridge: Cambridge University Press, 1981), pp. 187–90

❖

WALLACE FOWLIE ON THE VOYAGE THEME IN DANTE

[Wallace Fowlie (b. 1908), a poet, novelist, translator, and critic, has taught at Yale University, the University of Chicago, Bennington College, and Duke University. Among his many books are *Age of Surrealism* (1950), *Mallarmé* (1953), and *A Reading of Proust* (1964). In this extract from his book on the *Inferno* (1981), Fowlie asserts that the central motif of the *Inferno*—a voyage on both the literal and the metaphorical levels—is one of the oldest in literature.]

Dante's voyage to God goes through the world first. The circles of Hell, as conceived by the poet, are the scenes of human existence, but as they will be forever. The horrors of the world have to be experienced before one can move beyond them to the non-worldly joys of Purgatory and Paradise. All the forms of incontinence and malice have to be known in their terrestrial settings before the voyager can move to the world beyond them.

At the very beginning of the poem, Dante is in distress; a messenger, Virgil, comes to help him. But we learn in the second canto that this is no chance encounter. Virgil has been sent by Beatrice, who is among the blessed. Beatrice had been sent by Lucia, Dante's patron saint, who in turn had been spoken to by Mary, the queen of Heaven. Four intermediaries have been solicited to help Dante, since he could no longer help himself. His voyage, taking its point of departure on earth and going first through Hell, has therefore an absolute beginning in

Heaven, where Mary, not named as such, but called a noble lady (*Donna è gentil nel ciel*), is the link with the divine mystery that sets everything in motion.

Dante will never be left alone, from the moment of the appearance of Virgil, who will lead him through all the phases and all the experiences of sin. These experiences are never cut off from the world. A historical reality surrounds them, which at the same time is depicted so as to appear eternal. The words *eterno* and *eternità* resound throughout the eternal regions. Everywhere on this voyage one is sensitive to a great change, the mutation of men passing from time into eternity. All the spirits, either historical or legendary, whom Dante meets and talks with, once walked on the earth.

Dante was not obsessed by time as Proust was. His power as a poet is in seizing time and inventing for it a pulsation that beats in the present. He puts together a structure for time. Proust, on the other hand, is time's victim. The descent in *A la recherche du temps perdu* is not into Hell—Proust is there already—but a universal descent into the void. Because of life's fluidity and ephemeral nature, death is real for Proust. The metamorphosis that death will bring is simply a mask for the degradation of life. Dante, who has no dread of time, no obsession with it, would call it that force that assassinates and, ironically, sustains life and promotes it.

Dante's motif is one of the oldest in literature: a voyage through the world beyond the world. Homer narrates one in the eleventh book of the *Odyssey*, in which Odysseus descends to the underworld in order to learn from Tiresias whether it will be granted to him to return to his wife and native land. Virgil, too, narrates one in the sixth book of the *Aeneid*, where we see Aeneas going to the underworld so that the ghost of his father Anchises will reveal to him his destiny. These two voyages of antiquity, both of which were known to Dante, demonstrate the belief that the dead know more about life than the living. The dead, in a word, are more powerful than the living.

Between the fourteenth and twentieth centuries, how, if at all, has man's history changed? In a general sense, it is not difficult to make the transition from the dead in the underworld regions of Homer and Virgil, and the damned souls in Dante's *Inferno,* to the descent into the subterranean cosmos of personality which one can achieve today, especially at moments of great life crisis when we need to consult the dead of our race who still live in us, and the dead figures of our own personality who desire to return to the living self and resume an interrupted existence.

The subconscious is endless and as deep as Dante makes his Hell. It is filled with as many grimacing and sad and violent figures as those that we encounter in the Italian poem. The speech of the lost figures in our own life is as enigmatical, dramatic, and elliptical as the speech of Filippo Argenti, Farinata, and Cavalcante, father of Guido Cavalcanti. In the circles of his Hell, Dante encounters ghosts of the past who bear some relation to his own moral scruples and defects, as today an individual encounters, in successive medical consultations and self-analyses, the origins of his conflicts.

Dante's spirits and the realms they inhabit are graphically portrayed. Only the size of these realms is incommensurable with the earth and hard for the reader to grasp. It is the difference between earth and eternity, and yet Dante keeps reminding his readers that it is on earth that man's eternal existence is determined. Everything on the earth is eternalized once life ends. This is in keeping with the defects and trials and devastations that are prolonged and eternalized for us through our very distant and very immediate pasts. The funnel of Dante's Hell constitutes a landscape of sin, which today in our more tentative and more evasive language we call "obsessions."

The map of Hell, both that which precedes and that which makes up the city of Dis, is the map of the heart turned against itself, which in its freedom has turned away from freedom's source, namely, the love of God. The reader is bewildered and even depressed by the number of sins that Dante shows us in action, each sin undoing itself. But Dante never meant us to believe that a single soul commits all of the sins. However, since the poet's focus is on the city, the *città dolente,* on a society affected by all individual sins, he has to show all of them within a single image. Dis is therefore the image of the city perverted. At the summit of Paradise, it will appear in the form of a yellow rose.

First, the voyager has to move downward. Hell is a funnel sucking him in, and it can begin anywhere, in a dark forest, for example. Before one knows it, one is sucked into all the possibilities of depravity. The slightest turning away from the good, the slightest indulgence in self-knowledge, will lead to a more deliberate, serious turning away. This is the story of Dante's *Inferno*, and the story behind most individual lives.
—Wallace Fowlie, *A Reading of Dante's* Inferno (Chicago: University of Chicago Press, 1981), pp. 5–7

TEODOLINDA BAROLINI ON VIRGIL

[Teodolinda Barolini (b. 1951), a professor of Italian at Columbia University, is the author of *The Undivine Comedy: Detheologizing Dante* (1992) and *Dante's Poets* (1984), from which the following extract is taken. Here, Barolini examines the figure of Virgil, showing that he undergoes a metamorphosis in the course of the poem.]

It is no secret that Dante's imitation of the *Aeneid* decreases as the *Comedy* progresses. Whitfield points out that of the two hundred uses of Vergil claimed by Moore, "90 of these passages concern the *Inferno*, 34 the *Purgatorio*, and 13 the *Paradiso*, while the rest are scattered in Dante's other writings." Petrocchi establishes a pattern of inverse relation between Dante's use of translations from the *Aeneid* and his use of translations from the Bible: while translations from the Roman text occur seven times in the *Inferno*, five times in the *Purgatorio*, and only once in the *Paradiso*, translations from the Christian text occur twelve times in the *Paradiso*, eight times in the *Purgatorio*, and only twice in the *Inferno*. The *Inferno* is thus Vergil's canticle, dominated by his presence and saturated with his text. Nonetheless, despite Vergil's very real preeminence in the first canticle, he is not immune from an implicit critique even within its bounds; in other words, he does not lose his authority all at once, at the beginning of the *Purgatorio* when Cato rebukes him, but in a more subtle fashion, step by step from the moment he enters the poem. When Vergil arrives an hourglass is set, and the grains of sand fall one by one until, in *Purgatorio* XXX, the glass is empty.

The stature that the text will work to diminish must first be established, at the poem's outset: in canto I, where Vergil's authority is unassailable, even in his evident exclusion; in canto II, where Beatrice initiates, with reference to the Latin poet, the use of the *captatio benevolentiae* tied to the theme of earthly fame; in canto III, which openly adopts the mechanisms of the Vergilian afterlife for the *Comedy;* and in canto IV, where Vergil is hailed by his august comrades. If *Inferno* III contains more crude Vergilian echoes than any other canto in the poem, *Inferno* IV less blatantly evokes the *Aeneid;* the description of Limbo's "nobile castello," surrounded by its seven walls and dry riverbed, is reminiscent of the symbolic architecture and topography found in *Aeneid* VI. Dante seems to be deliberately imitating a mode whose trappings he will gradually shed as the exigencies of his own art take over, as though to underscore the point that after joining the classical poets and becoming one of their fraternity, he will keep on going, leaving them behind. Dramatically, the relation between Vergil and his charge in these first cantos is a formal one: if we consider the use of the emblematic nouns assigned to Vergil at the end of canto II, in the verse "tu duca, tu segnore e tu maestro" ("You the leader, you the lord, and you the master" [140]), we note that Vergil is regularly called *buon maestro* and *duca mio,* without any additional affective terminology; he is also referred to simply as *poeta.* The tenor of the rapport between the pilgrim and his guide during the first stage of their journey is best summed up by the recurrent expressions denoting absolute confidence in Vergil's judgment and understanding: he is all-knowing ("quel savio gentil, che tutto seppe" "that gentle sage, who knew all" [*Inf.* VII, 3]), and the sea of all wisdom ("E io mi volsi al mar di tutto 'l senno" "And I turned to the sea of all wisdom" [*Inf.* VIII, 7]).

Interestingly, both these hyperbolic tributes to Vergil's wisdom precede the encounter with the devils at the gates of Dis, the first episode to seriously call into question Vergil's abilities as guide. When Dante turns to Vergil, "al mar di tutto 'l senno," he does so in order to ask his guide the meaning of the signals being exchanged by the Stygian watchtowers, signals that effectively mark the beginning of a series of events whose culmination will be the advent of the heavenly intercessor toward the end of canto IX. The pilgrim's query is followed by the arrival of the boatman Phlegyas, who eventually deposits the travelers at the entrance to Dis; it is preceded by a unique instance of flashback in the *Comedy's* narration: although Dante and Vergil arrive at the foot of a tower in the last verse of canto VII, canto VIII begins by explaining that long before they had arrived at the tower they saw the exchange of signals between it and a more distant companion. Rather than minimize this narrative occurrence, the poet does everything in his power to emphasize it, opening canto VIII with a self-conscious insistence on both the new beginning and the use of flashback: "Io dico, seguitando, ch'assai prima / che noi fossimo al piè de l'alta torre" ("I say, continuing, that long before we had arrived at the foot of the high tower" [*Inf.* VIII, 1–2]). In fact, canto VIII's exordium is so pronounced that in order to account for it the early commentators came up with a biographical explanation, according to which Dante composed the first seven cantos of the *Inferno* before his exile and returned to canto VIII after a long interruption. Even more unusual than the exposed narrative link, "Io dico, seguitando," is the retrograde narration, which causes Benvenuto to comment that the author here "turns back in an artificial order." I would suggest that these narrative jolts are deliberately employed by Dante in order to mark an ideological jolt, indeed a crucial ideological turning point: namely, the moment in which we begin to realize that Vergil is not infallible, nor, as he has been viewed up to now, the fount of all wisdom.

—Teodolinda Barolini, *Dante's Poets: Textuality and Truth in the Comedy* (Princeton: Princeton University Press, 1984), pp. 201–4

JOAN M. FERRANTE ON POLITICAL AND SOCIAL ASPECTS OF HELL

[Joan M. Ferrante (b. 1936) is a professor of English at Columbia University and author of *Woman as an Image in Medieval Literature* (1975), *Dante's Beatrice: Priest of an Androgynous God* (1992), and other works. In this extract from her study of Dante's political vision, Ferrante finds Dante's Hell to be representative of contemporary political and social evils.]

The proper relation of individual states (cities or kingdoms) to the empire and the separate and distinct functions of ecclesiastical and secular authority discussed in chapters one and two provide the political framework for the *Comedy*. Within that framework, each cantica presents a different but related model for human society. Paradise is the ideal society in all its essential elements working harmoniously; Purgatory is a society in transition, moving from self-centeredness to concern for and commitment to others, but not yet organized within an effective structure. Hell reveals what society is when all its members act for themselves and against the common good. The souls here are condemned not just for their selfish motivations but also for the effects of their actions on others. Dante's point is that as civic beings, we are responsible not only for our actions, but also for their results. The people he presents were all men and women of prestige and/or power, people in a position to influence others either directly or by example, and in one way or another they all failed. The suffering, the violence, the anarchy of Hell are a result of their failure to act up to their responsibilities or their outright abuse of those responsibilities. Selfishness, greed for money, power, or pleasure, is the basis of the injustice that reigns in Hell, as charity is the basis of the justice that operates in heaven.

Bonaventure and Aquinas name four objects of love or sin: God, ourselves, our neighbors, and our bodies; Dante adds a fifth, our community. It is not that the theologians are not concerned with the effects of our actions on others, but that they are not primarily concerned with the public aspect of those actions, with their consequences for society as an entity. Dante, in contrast, shows how all sins contribute to social disorder, not only the overtly disruptive sins of violence, fraud, and treachery but even those that seem most personal. Lust, gluttony, greed have sociopolitical overtones; even heresy and suicide are presented within a political context. Barratry (graft within the government) is placed in a lower section than simony (graft in the church) because corruption within the state has a greater effect on society; both are treated as aspects of fraud, that is, as social rather than religious sins. Flattery and hypocrisy are lower than robbery and murder (except for murder committed by treachery), not because in themselves Dante considers them more serious sins, but because their effects on society are more insidious and ultimately more damaging. Dante reverses Aquinas's consideration of theft and robbery: for Aquinas, theft, which is secret, is not as bad as robbery, which is open and violent and does more physical harm to its victim. The secrecy is what makes theft worse for Dante, since it opens the way to various kinds of injustice, like the incrimination of the innocent, and threatens economic stability in a much graver way. For Aquinas, blasphemy is also worse than murder or theft because it is a direct attack on God, but Dante places blasphemy in the seventh circle, theft far below it in the seventh section of the eighth circle.

The most serious sins for Dante are those that deny the trust on which social and political relations are based—fraud and treachery. Although treachery is the worst of all because of the special relation between "perpetrator" and victim, fraud is the one that occupies Dante's attention. He devotes thirteen cantos (from 18 to 30) to it, more than a third of Hell, and he subdivides it into ten different sections. It is not unusual to subdivide sins; the capital vices are normally discussed in terms of the sins they spawn. But Dante differs in two ways from others who make the distinctions; (1) he presents the first five sins without any real subdivisions, (2) he moves into three sins which would normally be offshoots of others, violence, fraud, and treachery, and subdivides them, violence into three sections (the second with two parts, the third with three), fraud into ten (the tenth with four parts), and treachery into four. By introducing all these complexities, he is clearly calling attention to these sins, forcing us to shift the emphasis from the traditional moral view of greed and pride as the worst of evils to the more sociopolitical distinctions of violence, fraud, and treachery. The cantica seems to draw more from legal codes than manuals on vice; several of the punishments, particularly in the eighth circle, are based on contemporary penal codes. The very concept of Dante's Hell peopled with sinners well known to Dante's audience may itself be a reflection of the contemporary practice of painting the portraits of certain criminals on the walls of public buildings.

— Joan M. Ferrante, *The Political Vision of the* Divine Comedy (Princeton: Princeton University Press, 1984), pp. 132–35

Alison Morgan on the Classification of Sin

[Alison Morgan (b. 1930) is the author of *Dante and the Medieval Other World* (1990), from which the following extract is taken. Here, Morgan studies the classification of sin in the *Inferno* in the context of theological thought in the Middle Ages.]

An analysis of the classification of sin in the visions of the other world from the first to the twelfth centuries reveals a process of gradual change. Greater prominence is given to different sins in different periods: the most frequently cited sins in the New Testament lists are fornication, murder, and evil thoughts or speech. In the apocrypha they become jointly slander, sorcery, persecution, deceit, murder and blasphemy. The early medieval texts stress murder, avarice, deceit, the sowing of discord and theft. In the twelfth century the most common are adultery, lust, theft, and murder.

Further analysis shows that not only do the principal sins change; others are added, or receive greater emphasis. For example, the apocrypha add several sins which are found through to the twelfth-century texts: these are usury, loss of faith or backsliding, loss of chastity in unmarried women, and insincere alms-giving. In the early medieval visions much greater emphasis is placed on theft and the sowing of discord than previously; and in the twelfth century increased prominence is given to treachery, tyranny, pride and gluttony. From the staring point of the ten commandments and the lists given in the New Testament, with the further expansion which occurred initially as the first penitentials were composed and subsequently during the period of the confession manuals, a climax is reached in the twelfth-century visions. At this point the list of sins reaches its greatest length; forty distinct categories occur in the texts analysed.

The degree of similarity between the sins listed in texts of various periods and the *Inferno* becomes apparent when a more detailed comparison is made. Infractions of all ten commandments are punished in Dante's Hell with the sole exception of the fourth, to honour the sabbath. The seven New Testament passages list a total of some thirty-two sins, in order of frequency as follows: fornication, murder, evil thoughts or speech, idolatry, avarice, deceit, impurity, sorcery, foolishness, blasphemy, adultery, theft, pride, quarrelling, envy, drunkenness/gluttony, homosexuality, wickedness, malice and injustice (mentioned in two or more passages), and timidity, unbelief, slander/gossip, evil deeds, disobedience to parents, disorderliness, lust, anger, schism, rivalry, lack of affection and lack of mercy (mentioned only once). These texts make no attempt to classify the sins listed in any way, but it is immediately apparent that the majority of the aims themselves are identical to those represented in the *Inferno.* This suggests that although the New Testament cannot have influenced Dante's classificatory system, his choice of sins to include within that system must have sprung ultimately from the Christian rather than from the Aristotelian tradition.

Such a supposition receives further confirmation if a detailed comparison is made between the sins included in the popular Christian representations of the other world and those of the *Inferno.* The best known of these representations is perhaps the *Vision of Paul,* implied by Dante's son Jacopo to have been known to his father. What is particular about the vision is that, in contrast to the majority of the popular representations of the afterlife, many different redactions and translations were made throughout the medieval period, and taken together these give us a panorama of the various sins punished in the popular other world over a number of centuries. ⟨. . .⟩ All the Dantean sins are represented with the exception of anger and sloth (circle five), suicide, blasphemy and homosexuality (circle seven) and simony (circle eight).

The same pattern emerges if we compare the sins represented in the twelfth-century visions, plus that of Thurkill, with those of the *Inferno*. There are also two texts which do not properly belong to the Western tradition of vision literature, both dating from the thirteenth century: the Eastern *Liber de Scalis* and the verse description of the infernal city of Babylon by Bonvesin da Riva; both these give a classification of sin and have therefore been included. These texts together list a total of some forty-two sins, the most frequent of which are: adultery, lust, murder, theft, robbery, fornication, pride, avarice, gluttony, worldliness, tyranny, divination, abortion, treachery, sacrilege, slander, deceit, hatred, simony, false witness, heresy/unbelief, harm of others, injustice, fraud, indifference, hypocrisy, pandering, sodomy, perjury, envy, usury, idolatry, the sowing of discord, flattery and negligence. As with the *Vision of Paul,* all these are present in the *Inferno* with the exceptions of envy and pride, which are placed by Dante in Purgatory, and abortion, which is usually linked in the visions with divination, punished in the fifth ditch of circle eight in the *Inferno.* The others either have direct equivalents in the *Inferno* or are subsumed into other categories. ⟨. . .⟩

A similar correspondence can be found between the sins represented in the *Inferno* and those listed in the thirteenth-century confession manuals, although the manuals give a much more detailed breakdown of the forms of each sin than the *Comedy.* The manuals classify sins according to the seven capital vices or the ten commandments, and include almost all those punished in Dante's Hell. Under avarice, for example, the *Summa vitiorum* of Guglielmus Paraldus, written between 1250 and 1260, lists among others usury, robbery, fraud, simony and prodigality, and under lust, seduction, adultery and homosexuality. ⟨. . .⟩

In conclusion, then, the thirty-seven sins punished in the *Inferno* are essentially the same sins as those traditionally represented in the popular visions of the other world and listed in the confession manuals of the twelfth and thirteenth centuries. The existence of these correspondences would seem to confirm the suspicion raised by the inconsistencies in Dante's classificatory scheme that the classification of sin in the *Inferno* cannot simply be regarded as an outworking of the broad Aristotelian categories given in *Inferno* XI. Far from constituting surprising enigmas in an original system structured around the distinctions of incontinence, malice and bestiality, the complexities, inconsistencies and ambiguities in the classification of the *Inferno* bear witness to the mass of traditional material which lies behind it and determines its constituent parts. Support is given to this hypothesis by the fact that although taken individually the later visions identify many more sins than the earlier texts, the overall number of sins listed at various periods in the development of the popular Christian tradition and in the *Comedy* remains fairly constant—approximately thirty-two in the New Testament passages taken together, thirty-nine in the medieval redactions of the *Vision of Paul,* forty in the twelfth-century visions and thirty-seven in the *Inferno* (numbers are approximate because of differences in vocabulary and because of the existence of subcategories of sin).

—Alison Morgan, *Dante and the Medieval Other World* (Cambridge: Cambridge University Press, 1990), pp. 129–31

GIUSEPPE MAZZOTTA ON THE ENCYCLOPEDIC NATURE OF *THE DIVINE COMEDY*

[Giuseppe Mazzotta (b. 1942) is a professor of Italian at Yale University. He is the author of *Dante, Poet of the Desert: History and Allegory in* The Divine Comedy (1979) and *The Worlds of Petrarch* (1993) and the editor of *Critical Essays on Dante* (1991). In this extract from *Dante's Vision and the Circle of Knowledge* (1993), Mazzotta explores the encyclopedic nature of *The Divine Comedy*.]

It has long been acknowledged that the *Divine Comedy* is a poetic encyclopedia or a *summa medievalis*. This conventional view of the poem's encyclopedism is still restated in our own time, and it can even be said to account for the scholarly recognition of the necessity of tools such as the *Enciclopedia dantesca* or the sundry general dictionaries and interdisciplinary volumes meant to provide bald summaries of the themes, concerns, and characters the poem draws from the most disparate sciences. But the definition of the poem's encyclopedic compass is hardly new.

One could mention Guido da Pisa's suggestion that the *Divine Comedy* is best figured by Noah's ark, or Benvenuto da Imola's sense of the poem's "ineffable abundance," which he attributes to the fact that "poetry is counted among the liberal arts because it surpasses all of them and embraces them all together; it excels by rising above all of them." The statement reappears with a slight but significant variation in Cristoforo Landino's preamble to his commentary on Dante. In his preliminary musings on the divine origin of poetry Landino marvels at Dante's (and the other ancient poets') "profound and various doctrine," Yet poetry, he says, cannot merely be classified "as one of those arts the ancients called liberal," because it is something "much more divine" than the liberal disciplines, for it "embraces them all." These assessments—which clearly depend on contrasting theoretical principles—constitute the vital focus and the foundation of the critical traditions on the *Divine Comedy,* and they find an extension in the views of, say, Gravina and Vico, who stress, respectively, the poem's rational encyclopedic structure and its sublime visionariness. But they are of some importance also because, taken together, they point to a sense of disjunction and disparity between classical questions of the poem's logical and rational order and, on the other hand, the problematics of poetic visionariness.

The encyclopedism of the *Divine Comedy* cannot be viewed only as a mere descriptive formula of its complexity, comprehensiveness, and cosmic scale; this view of the poem invests, on the contrary, the interpretive debates on Dante's sense of the value, extension, and limits of the sciences and philosophy; on the relationship between knowledge and desire; and on his lucid understanding of poetry as the breath, as it were, of all knowledge. There is still a strain of Dante criticism, represented by critics who, in the wake of Benedetto Croce, choose to bracket the theological and doctrinal substance of Dante's poetic thought in the assumption that the essence of poetry lies outside the structure of ideas and of systems of thought, and is only an intuitive matter of subjective taste or narrative craft. This traditional skepticism about structure and ideology notwithstanding, the concerns with knowledge are constant in Dante's imaginative world.

The narrative of the *Vita nuova* plunges the reader into the depths of the lover's inwardeness and of the nearly destructive excesses of a self-consciousness largely unanchored from the external world. *Convivio,* though left unfinished, tells the story of a philosophical quest for ethical values, and its metaphysical ground is Aristotle's generalized assertion from *Metaphysics* (I,i) that all men naturally desire to know, for knowlege, Dante adds, is the ultimate perfection of the soul. The seven liberal arts are duly acknowledged and placed within a planetary context, but the pursuit of this knowledge is carried out through philosophy, which is to be understood as the "love of wisdom," according to a standard definition, as the mind's effort to grasp all things, visible and invisible. The longing for knowledge, the value of reason as a guide on the path to vision, the tragically deluded transgressions committed to arrive at knowledge (the fall of Adam is a fall into knowledge as guilt—cf. *Par.* XXVI, 114–42), the morass of sophistry, and other motifs are massively intertwined in the fabric of the *Divine Comedy.*

—Giuseppe Mazzotta, *Dante's Vision and the Circle of Knowledge* (Princeton: Princeton University Press, 1993), pp. 15–16

Books by Dante

Italian texts:

Canzone. 1463.

La Divina Commedia. 1472.

Convivio. 1490.

De Vulgari Eloquentia. 1577.

Monarchia. 1740.

Opere. Ed. Pompeo Venturi et al. 1757–58. 4 vols. in 5.

Amori et rime. 1823.

Opere Minori. Ed. Pietri Fraticelli. 1834–40. 3 vols. in 6.

Epistole edite ed inedite. Ed. Alessandro Torri. 1842.

Opere Latine. Ed. Giambattista Giuliani. 1878–82. 2 vols.

Tutte le opere. Ed. Edward Moore. 1897. 3 vols.

Opere. Ed. Michele Barbi et al. 1921.

Opere (Edizione Nazionale). Ed. Giorgio Petrocchi. 1966. 4 vols.

Opere Minori. Ed. Domenico de Robertis and Gianfranco Contini. 1979. 2 vols. in 3.

La Divina Commedia. Ed. Tommaso di Salvo. 1985. 3 vols.

English translations:

The Divine Comedy. Tr. Henry Boyd. 1802. 3 vols.

The Vision; or, Hell, Purgatory, and Paradise. Tr. Henry Francis Cary. 1822. 2 vols.

Canzoniere. Tr. Charles Lyell. 1835.

The New Life. Tr. Charles Eliot Norton. 1859.

The Divine Comedy. Tr. Henry Wadsworth Longfellow. 1867. 3 vols.

The Divine Comedy. Tr. Charles Eliot Norton. 1891–92. 3 vols.

The New Life. Tr. Dante Gabriel Rossetti. 1899.

Latin Works. Tr. A. G. Ferrers Howell and Philip H. Wicksteed. 1904. 2 vols.

Dante and His Convivio. Tr. William Michael Rossetti. 1910.

The Divine Comedy. Ed. John D. Sinclair. 1939. 3 vols. (with Italian text).

The Portable Dante. Ed. Paolo Milano. 1947.

The Comedy. Tr. Dorothy L. Sayers and Barbara Reynolds. 1955–62. 3 vols.

Odes. Tr. H. S. Vere-Hodge. 1963.

The Divine Comedy. Ed. Charles S. Singleton. 1970–75. 6 vols. (with Italian text and commentary).

Works about Dante and the *Inferno*

Abrams, Richard. "Inspiration and Gluttony: The Moral Context of Dante's Poetics of the 'Sweet New Style.'" *Modern Literary Notes* 91 (1976): 30–59.

Barbi, Michele. *Life of Dante.* Tr. Paul Ruggiers. Berkeley: University of California Press, 1954.

Barolini, Teodolinda. *The Undivine Comedy: Detheologizing Dante.* Princeton: Princeton University Press, 1992.

Bergin, Thomas G. *Dante.* Boston: Houghton Mifflin, 1965.

———. *Dante's Divine Comedy.* Englewood Cliffs, NJ: Prentice-Hall, 1971.

———. *From Time to Eternity: Essays on Dante's Divine Comedy.* New Haven: Yale University Press, 1967.

Botterill, Steven. *Dante and the Mystical Tradition.* Cambridge: Cambridge University Press, 1994.

Boyde, Patrick. *Perception and Passion in Dante's Comedy.* Cambridge: Cambridge University Press, 1993.

Cassell, Anthony K. *Dante's Fearful Art of Justice.* Toronto: University of Toronto Press, 1984.

Centenary Essays on Dante. Oxford: Clarendon Press, 1965.

Charity, A. C. *Events and Their Afterlife: The Dialectics of Christian Typology in the Bible and Dante.* Cambridge: Cambridge University Press, 1966.

Collins, James J. *Dante—Layman, Prophet, Mystic.* Staten Island, NY: Alba House, 1989.

———. *Pilgrim in Love: An Introduction to Dante and His Spirituality.* Chicago: Loyola University Press, 1984.

Cosmo, Umberto. *A Handbook to Dante Studies.* Tr. David Moore. Oxford: Basil Blackwell, 1960.

D'Antoni, Francesca Guerra. *Dante's Burning Sands: Some New Perspectives.* New York: Peter Lang, 1991.

Davis, Charles T. *Dante and the Idea of Rome.* Oxford: Clarendon Press, 1957.

————. "Dante's Vision of History." *Dante Studies* 93 (1975): 143–60.

De Sua, William J., ed. *A Dante Symposium in Commemoration of the 700th Anniversary of the Poet's Birth.* Chapel Hill: University of North Carolina Press, 1965.

Fergusson, Francis. *Dante.* London: Weidenfeld & Nicolson, 1966.

Ferrucci, Franco. *The Poetics of Disguise: The Autobiography of the Work in Homer, Dante, and Shakespeare.* Tr. Ann Dunnigan. Ithaca, NY: Cornell University Press, 1980.

Foster, Kenelm. *The Two Dantes and Other Studies.* Berkeley: University of California Press, 1977.

Freccero, John. *Dante: The Poetics of Conversion.* Cambridge, MA: Harvard University Press, 1986.

Gilson, Etienne. *Dante the Philosopher.* Tr. David Moore. New York: Sheed & Ward, 1949.

Grayson, Cecil, ed. *The World of Dante: Essays on Dante and His Times.* Oxford: Clarendon Press, 1980.

Higgins, David H. *Dante and the Bible: An Introduction.* Bristol: University of Bristol Press, 1992.

Holloway, Julia Bolton. *Twice-Told Tales: Brunetto Latino and Dante Alighieri.* New York: Peter Lang, 1993.

Holmes, George D. *Dante.* New York: Hill & Wang, 1980.

Jacoff, Rachel. *The Cambridge Companion to Dante.* Cambridge: Cambridge University Press, 1993.

Jacoff, Rachel, and Jeffrey T. Schnapp, ed. *The Poetry of Allusion: Virgil and Ovid in Dante's* Commedia. Stanford: Stanford University Press, 1991.

Kay, Richard. *Dante's Christian Astrology.* Philadelphia: University of Pennsylvania Press, 1994.

————. *Dante's Swift and Strong: Essays on* Inferno XV. Lawrence: Regents Press of Kansas, 1978.

Kelly, Henry Ansgar. *Tragedy and Comedy from Dante to Pseudo-Dante.* Berkeley: University of California Press, 1989.

Kleiner, John. *Mismapping the Underworld: Daring and Error in Dante's* Comedy. Stanford: Stanford University Press, 1994.

Limentani, Uberto, ed. *The Mind of Dante.* Cambridge: Cambridge University Press, 1965.

Masciandaro, Franco. *Dante as Dramatist.* Philadelphia: University of Pennsylvania Press, 1991.

Mazzaro, Jerome. *The Figure of Dante: An Essay on the* Vita nuova. Princeton: Princeton University Press, 1981.

Mazzeo, Joseph Anthony. *Medieval Cultural Tradition in Dante's* Comedy. Westport, CT: Greenwood Press, 1960.

Mazzocco, Angelo. *Linguistic Theories in Dante and the Humanists.* Leiden: E. J. Brill, 1993.

Mazzotta, Giuseppe. *Dante, Poet of the Desert: History and Allegory in the* Divine Comedy. Princeton: Princeton University Press, 1979.

————. *Dante's Vision and the Circle of Knowledge.* Princeton: Princeton University Press, 1993.

Montano, Rocco. *Dante's Thought and Poetry.* Chicago: Gateway, 1988.

Parker, Deborah. *Commentary and Ideology: Dante in the Renaissance.* Durham, NC: Duke University Press, 1993.

Priest, Paul. *Dante's Incarnation of the Trinity.* Ravenna: Longo, 1982.

Reade, W. H. V. *The Moral System of Dante's* Inferno. Oxford: Clarendon Press, 1909.

Sayers, Dorothy L. *Further Papers on Dante.* New York: Harper & Brothers, 1957.

Schettino, Franco, ed. *A Dante Profile.* Los Angeles: University of Southern California Press, 1967.

Shapiro, Marianne. "The Fictionalization of Bertran de Born (*Inferno* 27)." *Dante Studies* 92 (1974): 107–16.

Shoaf, R. A. *Dante, Chaucer, and the Currency of the Word: Money, Images, and Reference in Late Medieval Poetry.* Norman, OK: Pilgrim Books, 1983.

Singleton, Charles S. *An Essay on the* Vita nuova. Cambridge, MA: Harvard University Press, 1958.

———. *Journey to Beatrice.* Cambridge, MA: Harvard University Press, 1957.

Tambling, Jeremy. *Dante and Difference: Writing in the Commedia.* Cambridge: Cambridge University Press, 1988.

Thompson, David. "Figure and Allegory in the *Commedia.*" *Dante Studies* 90 (1972): 1–11.

Vittorini, Domenico. *The Age of Dante.* Syracuse: Syracuse University Press, 1957.

Whitbread, Leslie George. *Fulgentius the Mythographer.* Columbus: Ohio State University Press, 1971.

Williams, Charles. *The Figure of Beatrice: A Study in Dante.* New York: Farrar, Straus & Giroux, 1961.

Index of
Themes and Ideas